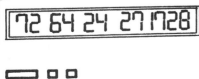

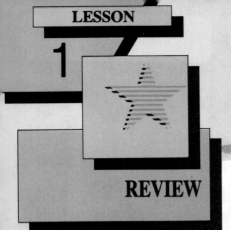

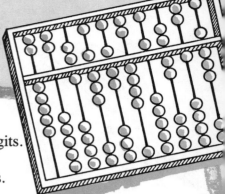

Place Value/ Bar Graphs

REVIEW

Large numbers are grouped in **periods** of three digits.
Units, thousands, and millions are **periods**.
Each period may contain ones, tens, and hundreds.

477,391,089 means 477 million, 391 thousand, 89

Look at these word codes.
SIT stands for 463,321,805.   **TOP** stands for 805,609,003.

The first letter in the word is the millions period. The second letter is the
thousands period. The third letter is the units period. Here are the word
codes for some letters.

S – 463	**O** – 609	**T** – 805	**I** – 321	**B** – 136
E – 80	**G** – 54	**P** – 3	**A** – 7	**N** –762

1. What numbers do the following words stand for?

   a. NOT _____   **b. BIN** _____ **c. SAT** _____

   d. SEA _____   **e. BEG** _____ **f. TOO** _____

2. Write the number that is:

   a. 20 million greater than **PIE** _____   **b.** 300 less than **PAT** _____

   c. 70 thousand greater than **SAG** _____   **d.** 5,000 greater than **TAG** _____

   e. 400,000,000 greater than **BIG** _____   **f.** Seventy less than **TIE** _____

Use the number line to find the answers to these questions.

A   B   C   D   E   F   G   H   I   J   K   L   M   N

1. If **C** is 100,000,000 and **E** is 200,000,000, then **G** is

_____,

I is _____, and **D** is _____.

2. Tell how you know which number goes with each letter. _____

_____

3. If **D** is 41,000,000 and **G** is 50,000,000, then

   a. 47,895,620 would be closer to which letter? _____

   b. 55,679,970 would be closer to which letter? _____

4. Place a mark and a letter on this number line where you think the number would be.

0   12,000,000   36,000,000

   A for 24,000,000, **B** for 5,000,000, and **C** for 18,000,000

5. Locate and mark each answer on this number line. Then label it.

0   250,000

   A for 1,000,000, **B** for 100,000 and **C** for 357,865

6. Explain how you decided where to place each number on the line. ____

_____

_____

PROBLEM SOLVING
Bar Graphs

1. In what year was the population about 180,000,000? _____

2. Do you think the population was exactly 180,000,000? _____
Why, or why not? _____
_____

3. Was the population of the United States in 1940 closer to 120 million or 140 million?
_____

4. What is your estimate for the population in 1940? _____

5. About how much did the population increase between 1960 and 1980?
_____

6. What steps did you use to find the answer? _____
_____

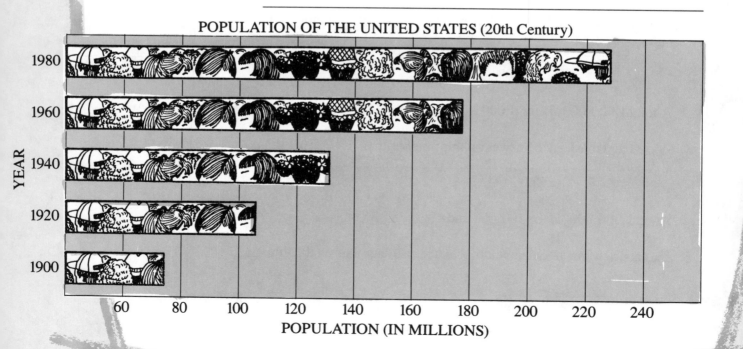

POPULATION OF THE UNITED STATES (20th Century)

YEAR

1980 | 1960 | 1940 | 1920 | 1900

POPULATION (IN MILLIONS)
60 80 100 120 140 160 180 200 220 240

6 Place value to 100 million; making and using a bar graph

Estimation can be used to gain more information from a graph.

Estimate the populations for years not listed on the graph.

7. What do you estimate the population was in 1950? Use the populations for 1940 and 1960 to help you.

_____

8. How did you decide on your estimate? _____

_____

9. What would you estimate the population was in 1945? _____

10. How did you arrive at that guess? _____

_____

11. Make a bar graph below, predicting the population in 2000 and 2020. Use the graph on the last page to help you.

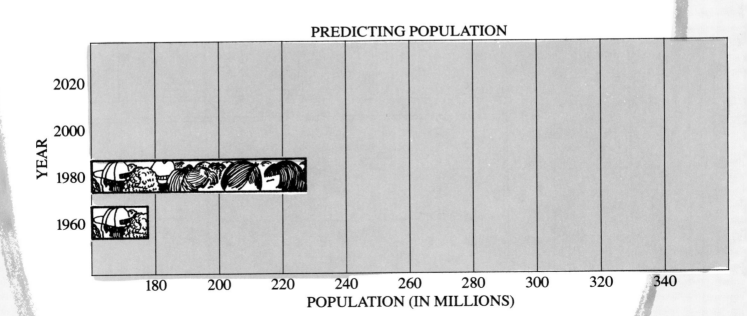

PREDICTING POPULATION

Round, Compare, and Order Numbers/Logical Reasoning

2,375,891   3,489,775   2,786,056

Order the numbers   2,375,891 < 2,786,056 < 3,489,775

2,375,891 rounded to the nearest hundred is 2,375,900
3,489,775 rounded to the nearest thousand is 3,490,000
2,782,056 rounded to the nearest ten thousand is 2,780,000

Round each number to the underlined digit.

1. 7<u>6</u>,784

_____

2. <u>1</u>28,306

_____

3. 3<u>8</u>1,294

_____

4. 9,<u>5</u>38

_____

5. 5,7<u>4</u>6,238

_____

6. 2<u>7</u>5,687

_____

7. <u>9</u>05,687

_____

8. <u>7</u>53,134

_____

9. 8<u>3</u>7,412

_____

10. 934,<u>7</u>83

_____

11. <u>4</u>56,099

_____

12. <u>7</u>,613

_____

13. The five greatest answers are:

_____ _____ _____ _____ _____

14. Write these five numbers in order.

Least   Greatest

Arrange all 5 digits to write numbers.

1. Write the number

   a. which rounds up when rounded to thousands but down when rounded to hundreds.

   _____

   b. which rounds down to tens but up to hundreds. _____

2. Write the greatest number which rounds down to thousands and hundreds.

   _____

3. Write the least number which rounds up to hundreds and down to tens.

   _____

POPULATION OF HAMPTON PLAINS TOPS 4,000,000

4. Look at the number in the headlines. Is there a number that rounds to this number when rounded to hundred thousands but not when rounded to millions?

   _____

5. If there is, write it here. _____

6. If there is not, explain why not. _____

   _____

   _____

PROBLEM SOLVING
Logical Reasoning

Roscoe loved to round numbers, but he could not always remember when to round them. Sometimes he rounded when he should not have. Sometimes he didn't round when he should have.

Roscoe's new teacher asked him for some information. He said his house number was around 1,200 on about 20th Street. He was born in nearly 2,000 A.D. and was 13 years 2 months and 13 days old. His telephone number was 5,000,000. He was 1,234 millimeters tall and weighed 0 kilograms. What a guy!

1. Is it likely that Roscoe lived at 1,200 on 20th Street? _____

2. Why or why not? _____

_____

3. If 1,200 and 20 are estimates, what are possible values for the address and street number?

House number from _____ to _____

Streets from _____ to _____

4. Did Roscoe round the date of his birth to the nearest ten, hundred, or thousand?

_____

5. If this interview took place recently, in what year was Roscoe actually born?

_____

6. He rounded his weight to the nearest 100 kilograms. What is the most he could weigh?

_____

7. If the telephone number was rounded to the nearest ten thousand what is the least the telephone number could be?

_____

8. 1,234 millimeters is a very small and accurate measure of height. Usually larger estimates are given for height. What would be a reasonable estimate for Roscoe's height?

_____

This is an article from a newspaper. Some numbers are rounded and should not be. Others are not rounded and should be. Rewrite the numbers choosing reasonable values.

TIP Read numbers in a paragraph with care. Concentrate on their meaning and importance.

> The United States Senate today approved a bill of $4,312,567.43 to aid deprived farmers. In nearly 20 states 32,467 farms will be effected by the bill. Debate on the bill was long and heated, lasting 8 hours, 52 minutes, and 43 seconds. The vote of the 100 senators on the bill was about 70 to 40. Many people feel that the cost of the bill will require taxes to be raised $198 for each of the 64,000,000 families in this country. This bill will take effect in about 1990.

9. Write reasonable estimates for these numbers from the story by rounding them.

    a. $4,312,567.43 _____

    b. 32,467 _____

    c. 8 hours, 52 minutes, and 43 seconds _____

    d. $198 _____

10. Write reasonable values for these rounded numbers from the story.

    a. 20 _____   **b.** 70 to 40 _____ to _____

    c. 64,000,000 _____   **d.** 1990 _____

Estimation/Guess and Check

Round to the greatest place value.
Then add.

$$4,572 \rightarrow 5,000$$
$$+6,320 \rightarrow +6,000$$
$$\overline{\hspace{1.2cm} 11,000}$$

Round to the greatest place value.
Then subtract.

$$8,975 \rightarrow 9,000$$
$$-3,409 \rightarrow -3,000$$
$$\overline{\hspace{1.2cm} 6,000}$$

Round the prices to the greatest place value. Write the rounded price on the hood of each car.

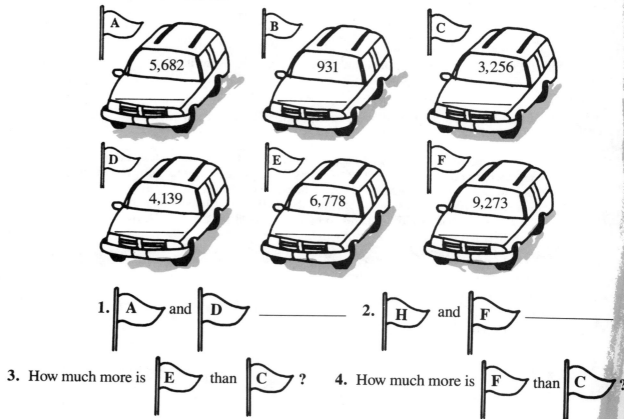

A 5,682   B 931   C 3,256

D 4,139   E 6,778   F 9,273

1. A and D _____

2. H and F _____

3. How much more is E than C ?

_____

4. How much more is F than C ?

_____

5. How much do cars C and D cost?

_____

6. How much less are E and B than F ?

_____

NEW CAR OPTION PACKAGES

Package A $ 3,678   Package B $ 6,783

Package C $ 2,805   Package D $ 2,239

1. Estimate the cost of packages **A** and **C**. _____

2. Do not find the actual sum. Is your estimate greater than or less than the actual cost?

   _____

3. How can you tell? _____

4. Estimate the difference between the cost of package **B** and the cost of package **D**.

   _____

5. Do not find the actual difference. Is your estimate greater than or less than the actual difference?

   _____

6. How do you know? _____

7. Estimate each answer. Then tell whether the estimated answer is greater than or less than the actual answer.

a.	**b.**	**c.**	**d.**
6,292	7,402	12,946	34,502
4,813	− 2,944	+34,476	− 27,894
+7,696			

   _____   _____   _____   _____

PROBLEM SOLVING
Guess and Check

Four 4-digit numbers are rounded to the nearest thousand and then added. The sum of the rounded numbers is 19,000. What are the greatest and least numbers the original numbers could have been?

 You may wish to use a calculator with these exercises.

1. Rounded number   **2.** Greatest number   **3.** Least number

_____   _____   _____

_____   _____   _____

_____   _____   _____

_____   _____   _____

4. Find the sum of the four numbers in exercise 2. _____

5. How do you know this is the greatest sum? _____

_____

6. Find the sum of the four numbers in exercise 3. _____

7. How do you know this is the least sum? _____

_____

You found the greatest and least numbers for the numbers you picked. Pick four different rounded numbers which have a sum of 19,000. Find the greatest and least number that rounds to each.

8. Rounded number   **9.** Greatest number   **10.** Least number

_____   _____   _____

_____   _____   _____

_____   _____   _____

_____   _____   _____

11. Find the sum of the greatest numbers. _____

12. Find the sum of the least numbers. _____

13. How do these sums compare to the sums in exercise 4 and exercise 6?

_____

14. How can you be sure that these are the greatest and least sums for any rounded numbers that have a sum of 19,000?

_____

15. Do you think the greatest and least sums will always be the same?

_____

Why? _____

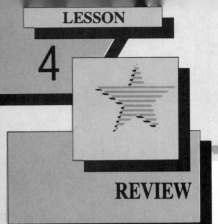

Addition and Subtraction/ One-Step Problems

Kevin's cat thought that the numbers on his math homework were tasty, so she ate them. Find the missing numbers or digits.

Kevin Kircher   5-2   Mrs. Jansen

1.   662,682
     +245,419
   ⬭

2.   459,823
     +257,127
   ⬭

3.   106,695
     +⬭
      586,127

4.   ⬭
    +647,898
     690,753

5.   676,126
    −237,842
   ⬭

6.   815,577
    −337,895
   ⬭

7.   403,016
    −⬭
    208,093

8.   ⬭
    −432,145
     467,935

9.   4,58◯
      23,6◯9
    +156,◯45
     184,313

10.   83,◯⬭
     +◯8,345
      542,313

11. 40◯,67◯
    −397,◯14
      8,3◯6

12. ◯83,5◯4
    −6◯1,◯99
     35◯,715

1. Using 4 of the digits 1, 2, 3, 4, 5, 6, 7, 8, 9, make this sum as great as you can. Place a different digit in each box.

$$\begin{array}{r} \square\square,267 \\ +\ \square\square,689 \\ \hline \end{array}$$

2. What is the greatest sum possible? _____

3. What two numbers did you add to make the greatest sum?

_____   _____

4. What is the least sum possible? _____

5. What two numbers did you add to make the least sum?

_____   _____

6. Select 4 of the digits 1, 2, 3, 4, 5, 6, 7, 8, 9, to make the difference. Place a different digit in each box.

$$\begin{array}{r} \square\square,846 \\ -\ \square\square,785 \\ \hline \end{array}$$

7. What is the greatest possible difference? _____

8. What two numbers did you use to get the greatest difference?

_____   _____

9. What is the least possible difference? _____

10. What two numbers did you use to make the least difference?

_____   _____

11. Find two other numbers that will give this difference.

_____   _____

12. Are there other pairs of numbers? Find and explain the pattern.

_____

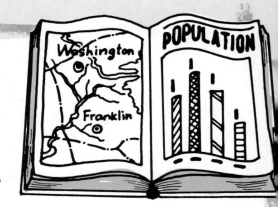

Washington and Franklin are two cities, both with populations greater than 435,000.

If the population of Washington is 12,380 greater than Franklin, what could be the populations of the two cities?

 **TIP** To solve a story problem find the information you need and decide which operation to use.

1. If the population of Franklin was 448,673, how would you find the population of Washington? _____

2. What would be the population of Washington? _____

3. If, instead, the population of Washington was 589,532, how would you find the population of Franklin?

   _____

4. What would be the population of Franklin? _____

5. Pick a different number for the population of Franklin. _____

6. What would be the population of Washington then? _____

7. Pick a different number for the population of Washington. _____

8. What would be the population of Franklin then? _____

9. What is the least the population of each city could be?

   _____   _____

The coach bought a used van for the basketball team. The cost was between $5,000 and $10,000. He gave the salesperson a check for $2,350.75. How much does he still owe?

10. If you knew the cost of the van, how would you find the amount the coach still owed?

_____

11. Find the greatest and the least amounts the coach could still owe on the van.
   a. Greatest amount the van could cost _____

   b. Amount the coach would owe _____

   c. Least amount the van could cost _____

   d. Amount the coach would owe _____

The odometer on the van reads between 37,000 and 40,000 miles now. The team has traveled 846 miles in the van.

12. What is the greatest reading the odometer could have had when it was purchased?

_____

13. What is the least reading the odometer could have had when it was purchased?

_____

Multiplication and Division/
Finding Information

Multiply or divide. Follow the trail. Use the answer to each problem in
the next problem.

START

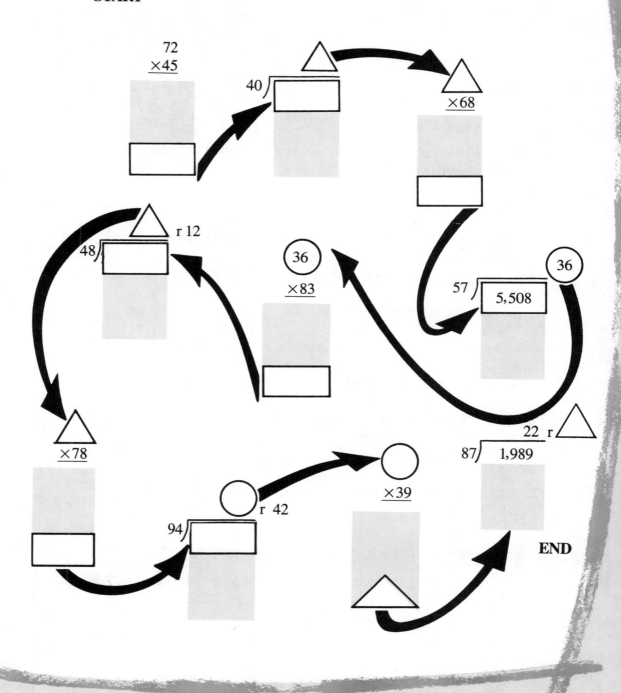

38 51 1,938

UNDERSTANDING

The following multiplication number sentences can be written using the numbers 38, 51, and 1,938.

$$38 \times 51 = 1,938 \qquad 51 \times 38 = 1,938$$

1. Write two division number sentences using the same three numbers.

_____   _____

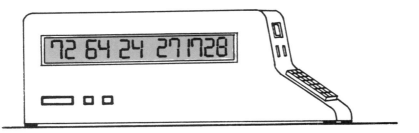

 You may wish to use a calculator for these exercises.

2. Write a multiplication sentence using three of the numbers above.

_____

3. Write a division sentence using three of the numbers above. Only one number can be the same as a number in exercise 2.

_____

4. Write a number sentence using 4 of the numbers above.

_____

5. Write a different number sentence using the same 4 numbers.

_____

6. Add any number you like to the above group. Write a number sentence using 5 numbers.

_____

PROBLEM SOLVING
Finding Information

At the Boston Tea Party the colonists raided one boat that had cases of tea stacked in layers. Each layer was 23 cases long and 34 cases wide. There were a total of 18 layers of cases.

1. Look at the paragraph above. List all the numbers and their labels.

   _____ _____ _____

 Breaking a problem into parts makes it easier to solve.

2. Using the numbers from exercise 1, list the additional information you can find.

   a. the number of cases in each layer   _____

   b. the total number of cases   _____

3. Forty-six colonists threw the tea into the harbor. If each threw in an equal number of cases, how many did each one throw? _____

4. If each case weighed 67 kilograms, what was the weight of the tea that each colonist threw into the bay? _____

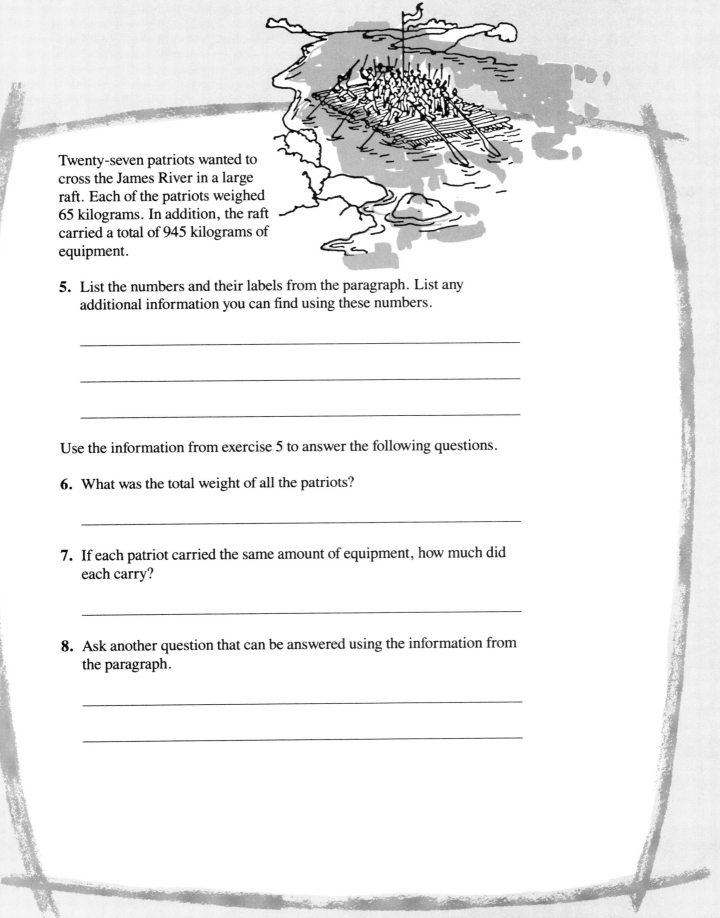

Twenty-seven patriots wanted to cross the James River in a large raft. Each of the patriots weighed 65 kilograms. In addition, the raft carried a total of 945 kilograms of equipment.

5. List the numbers and their labels from the paragraph. List any additional information you can find using these numbers.

_____

_____

_____

Use the information from exercise 5 to answer the following questions.

6. What was the total weight of all the patriots?

_____

7. If each patriot carried the same amount of equipment, how much did each carry?

_____

8. Ask another question that can be answered using the information from the paragraph.

_____

_____

Whole Number Computation/ Multi-Step Problems

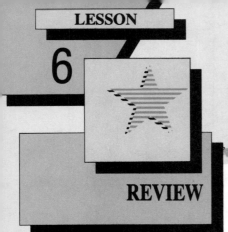

Find the answers.

1.

65,144   —   25,889

_____

2.

45   ×   63

_____

3.

3,476   ÷   67

_____

4.

57,934   17,320   76,543   +

_____

5.

6   7   85   ×

_____

6.

4,464   ÷   72

_____

7.

8,609   +   5,613   —   6,342

_____

8.

5,248   ÷   82   ×   36

_____

9.

56,007   —   38,693   +   98   ×

_____

1. Use the numbers 5,278, 3,460, and 1,558. Add the first two numbers and then subtract the third number from the answer.

   _____

2. Now subtract the second number from the first number and then add the third number.

   _____

3. Is the answer for exercise 2 different from the answer in exercise 1?

   _____

4. Why or why not? _____

5. Use the numbers 1,152, 24, and 6. Divide the first number by the second number and then divide that answer by the third number.

   _____

6. Now divide the second number by the third number. Then divide the first number by that answer.

   _____

7. Are the answers in exercises 5 and 6 equal?

   _____

8. Why or why not? _____

For exercises 9 and 10, use the numbers 952, 34, and 28.

9. **a.** Add, then multiply _____ **b.** Multiply, then add _____

10. **a.** Subtract, then divide _____ **b.** Divide, then subtract _____

11. Are the answers to each part of exercises 9 and 10 different? _____

12. Why? _____

PROBLEM SOLVING

Multi-Step Problems

The Yen family plans to rent a car for 3 days. The Madison Rent-A-Car Company charges $27.95 per day plus gasoline.

They plan to drive 975km. The car averages 13km per liter of gasoline.

The cost of the gasoline will average $.34 per liter. How much will the Yen family pay for the car rental and the gasoline?

 Breaking a problem into smaller parts makes it easier to solve.

1. What information can you get from the first two sentences?

_____

_____

_____

_____

2. What information can you get from the next two sentences?

_____

_____

_____

3. What is the total cost of the gasoline for the trip?

_____   **Show work here**

_____

4. What is the total cost of the car rental and the gasoline?

_____

_____

Show work here

Diana wants to save enough money to buy a stereo priced at $89.45. On her paper route she delivers 35 newspapers each Monday through Saturday and 40 newspapers on Sunday. She gets 3¢ for each daily paper and 12¢ for each Sunday paper she delivers. If she spends only $2.00 of her earnings each week, how many weeks will it take her to save enough money for the stereo?

5. Write down the information you know.

_____

_____

_____

_____

6. How much does she save each week?

_____

_____

7. How many weeks will it take to save enough money for the stereo?

_____

_____

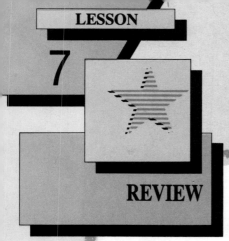
Elapsed Time/Draw a Diagram

Time now: 11:43 A.M.

Time in 37 minutes: 12:20 P.M.

Each of these students sets clocks differently.

Jason always
sets the clock
ahead 15 minutes.

Juan always
sets the clock
ahead 35 minutes.

Latisha always
sets the clock
back 40 minutes.

What time would these clocks show after the students reset them?

1.

Jason_____

2.

Juan_____

3.

Latisha_____

First one student reset the clock. Then other students did. Write the time
after each student reset the clock.

4.

a. Latisha_____

b. Jason_____

c. Juan_____

5.

a. Juan_____

b. Jason_____

c. Latisha_____

6.

a. Juan_____

b. Latisha_____

c. Jason_____

The minute hand on these clocks is missing. Guess what time it is.

1. a. What time is it? _____

    b. Why did you pick that time?

_____

_____

2. a. What time is it? _____

    b. Why did you pick that time?

_____

_____

3. a. Is the time before or

    after 4:30? _____

    b. Is it closer to
    4:00 or 4:30?

_____

    c. What is your guess? _____

4. a. Is the time before or

    after 10:30? _____

    b. Is it closer to
    10:30 or 11:00?

_____

    c. What is your guess? _____

5. What time is it? _____

6. What time is it? _____

PROBLEM SOLVING
Draw a Diagram

To what minute mark is
the hour hand pointing when
the time is 2:24?

Make a sketch of a clock. Fill in the minute marks between 1 and 6.
Show 2:00.

1. Now the hour hand points to 2. This is also the 10 minute mark.
How long before the hour hand points to the 15 minute mark?

_____

Drawing a diagram can help you solve problems.

2. How many minutes does it take the hour hand to move from the 10

minute mark to the 11 minute mark? _____

3. How did you find your answer? _____

_____

4. To what minute mark is the hour hand pointing at 2:24? _____

Jerri looks at a clock at exactly 8:00.
She looks at it again before 9:00.
The hands are on top of each other.
To the nearest minute, what time is it?

Draw a clock showing the minute marks between the 8 and the 9.

5. When the minute hand points to the 36 minute mark, to what

minute mark does the hour hand point? _____

6. How do you know that? _____

_____

7. To the nearest minute, what time is it when the hands are on top of
each other? Make another drawing to help you.

_____

8. How did you get your answer? _____

_____

_____

Cumulative Review

DIRECTIONS
Read each question. Choose the best answer. Then mark that answer in the space provided at the bottom of the page.

1 What number is 20,000,000 more than 43,567,345?

  A 45,567,345
  B 63,000,000
  C 63,567,345
  D 243,567,345
  E None of these

2 Round 567,893 to the nearest 10,000.

  F 600,000
  G 570,000
  H 560,000
  J 568,000
  K None of these

3 Which number would round up to 43,000 if rounded to the underlined digit?

  A 43,<u>7</u>78
  B 43,0<u>0</u>3
  C 4<u>3</u>,673
  D 4<u>3</u>,552
  E None of these

4 Estimate the difference to the nearest 10,000.

$$\begin{array}{r} 63,389 \\ -\ 34,467 \end{array}$$

  F 90,000
  G 40,000
  H 35,000
  J 45,000
  K None of these

5 The time is now 3:47 a.m. What time will it be in 55 minutes?

  A 4:42 a.m.
  B 4:37 a.m.
  C 4:32 a.m.
  D 4:02 a.m.
  E None of these

6 In 37 minutes the time will be 11:05 p.m. What time is it now?

  F 11:42 a.m.
  G 10:68 a.m.
  H 10:32 a.m.
  J 10:28 a.m.
  K None of these

1 Ⓐ Ⓑ Ⓒ Ⓓ Ⓔ
2 Ⓕ Ⓖ Ⓗ Ⓙ Ⓚ
3 Ⓐ Ⓑ Ⓒ Ⓓ Ⓔ

4 Ⓕ Ⓖ Ⓗ Ⓙ Ⓚ
5 Ⓐ Ⓑ Ⓒ Ⓓ Ⓔ
6 Ⓕ Ⓖ Ⓗ Ⓙ Ⓚ

Use this for exercises 7 and 8.

| A | B | C | D | E |

7 If A is 20,000,000 and D is 80,000,000, what is C?

   A 30,000,000
   B 40,000,000
   C 50,000,000
   D 60,000,000

8 If B is 15,000,000 and C is 18,000,000, between which letters should 22,893,456 lie?

   F D and E
   G C and D
   H B and C
   J A and B

9 Which number rounds up when rounded to hundreds and down when rounded to thousands?

   A 34,679
   B 36,479
   C 37,964
   D 39,764

10 Which of the following is false?

   F $28 \div 476 = 17$
   G $28 \times 17 = 476$
   H $476 = 17 \times 28$
   J $476 \div 17 = 28$

11 Which of the following problems will give an answer different from the others?

   A $2,312 \div 34 \div 68 =$
   B $2,312 \div 68 \div 34 =$
   C $2,312 \div 68 \times 34 =$
   D $64 \times 34 \div 2,312 =$

12 The hour is more than half way between 4 and 5. The time is:

   F 4:47
   G 5:03
   H 4:28
   J 4:15

7 Ⓐ Ⓑ Ⓒ Ⓓ
8 Ⓕ Ⓖ Ⓗ Ⓙ
9 Ⓐ Ⓑ Ⓒ Ⓓ

10 Ⓕ Ⓖ Ⓗ Ⓙ
11 Ⓐ Ⓑ Ⓒ Ⓓ
12 Ⓕ Ⓖ Ⓗ Ⓙ

Use this for exercises 13 and 14.

At the Kelvin Stadium there were 20 entrances and almost 5 parking lots. One Sunday 67,884 people bought 34,925 hot dogs and 83,403 cups of drink. The final score of the game was almost 40 to 20.

13 What would be the most reasonable way of reporting the number of entrances and parking lots?

   A Almost 20 and nearly 5
   B Just state the actual number of each.
   C More than 15 and less than 10
   D 25 altogether

14 What would be the most reasonable way of reporting the people and the hot dog and drink sales?

   F A total of 186,212 people, hot dogs and drinks
   G About 70,000 people bought 118,328 hot dogs and drinks.
   H About 70,000 people bought about 40,000 hot dogs and about 80,000 drinks.
   J About 70,000 people bought around 30,000 hot dogs and about 80,000 drinks.

15 Pedro had more than $1.00 and less than $2.00 in his pocket. He bought a malt for $.65. What is the most money he could have left?

   A You can't say for sure.
   B $1.35
   C $1.34
   D Less than $1.00

16 Patti bought ★ stamps each costing $.2★ cents and 2 envelopes each costing $.1★. The star represents an unknown number. If you knew the actual amounts, how would you determine the total Patti spent?

   F Add the cost of 3 stamps and the cost of 2 envelopes.
   G Add the cost of 3 stamps and multiply it by 2.
   H Add the cost of 1 stamp and the cost of 1 envelope, then multiply by 5.
   J Multiply the cost of 1 stamp by 3. Multiply the cost of 1 envelope by 2. Multiply those totals.

13 Ⓐ Ⓑ Ⓒ Ⓓ
14 Ⓕ Ⓖ Ⓗ Ⓙ

15 Ⓐ Ⓑ Ⓒ Ⓓ
16 Ⓕ Ⓖ Ⓗ Ⓙ

Use this for exercises 17, 18, and 19.

A movie theater had 24 seats in each row and a total of 32 rows. Each ticket cost $3.50. At the 6:00 show only 76 seats were empty.

17 What would you do first to find the total amount of money taken in at the 6:00 show?

   A Find the amount of money spent by 1 row.
   B Find the number of occupied seats.
   C Find the amount of money taken in if all the seats were occupied.
   D Find the total number of seats in the theater.

18 Which sentence would you choose to find the total number of occupied seats?

   F 24 × 32
   G 24 × 32 – $3.50
   H 24 × 32 – 76
   J 24 × 32 × $3.50

19 How much money was taken in at the 6:00 show?

   A $2684.00
   B $2422.00
   C $ 276.50
   D $ 242.20

20 Carrots are 3 for $.69 and Renae bought 6. Apples are 8 for $1.25 and she bought 16. Bananas are 4 for $.83 and she bought 8. How much money did she spend?

   F $5.54
   G $3.56
   H $2.77
   J $30.78

21 Eggs are $.72 a dozen and Martha bought 30 eggs. Apples are 2 for $.37 and Martha bought a dozen. Bananas are $.28 a pound and Martha bought some. If she spent $5.14, how many pounds of bananas did she buy?

   A 4
   B 8
   C 16
   D 43

17   Ⓐ Ⓑ Ⓒ Ⓓ
18   Ⓕ Ⓖ Ⓗ Ⓙ
19   Ⓐ Ⓑ Ⓒ Ⓓ

20   Ⓖ Ⓗ Ⓙ
21   Ⓑ Ⓒ Ⓓ

Round and Order Decimals/ Logical Reasoning

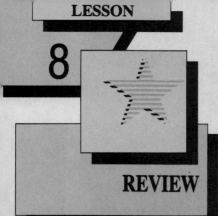

Round decimals to tenths. Look at the hundredths place. If 5 or greater, round up. If less, round down.

6.76 rounds to 6.8

Compare decimals. Line up decimal points. Start at the left. Compare each place.

5.38   5.38
4.92   5.6
5.6

4.92 is the least
5.6 is the greatest

1. Rounded to tenths I'm 3.2.
Rounded to ones I'm 3.
Write three numbers I could be.

_____ _____ _____

2. Rounded up to tenths I'm 4.5.
Rounded to ones I'm 4.
Write three numbers I could be.

_____ _____ _____

3. Rounded to tenths I'm 7.7.
Rounded to ones what am I?

_____

4. Rounded to tenths I'm 6.4.
Rounded down to ones I'm 6.
Write three numbers I could be.

_____ _____ _____

For exercises 5 and 6, write the numbers in order from least to greatest.

5. I am 0.6 greater than 2.17.
I am twice 1.15.
I am halfway between 2.3 and 2.4.

_____ _____ _____

6. I am 0.4 greater than 3.26.
I am 0.2 less than 5.78.
I am 0.7 greater than 4.33.

_____ _____ _____

7. Use the digits 5, 9, 2 to make a decimal like ☐.☐☐

I am the greatest. _____.

I am the least. _____.

I am the middle number.
_____.

8. Make a decimal like ☐.☐☐
I am the third greatest using the digits 4, 6, and 7. _____.

I am the second least using the digits 8, 9, 0.

_____.

1. Explain why you would round 4.509 to 4.5 when rounding to the nearest **tenth** and to 4.51 when rounding to the nearest **hundredth.**

_____ _____

_____

_____

2. Which numbers expressed in hundredths can be rounded to 8.7?

_____

_____

3. Write these numbers in order from greatest to least: 6.7, 6.58, 6.129, 6.09, 6.584. Explain each step you take as you put the numbers in order.

_____

_____

_____

_____

4. Pick five numbers. Round each one to a place of your choosing. Order the five numbers. Then order the rounded numbers. Try to choose so that at least 3 of the rounded numbers will be in a different order from your starting numbers.

Number _____ _____ _____ _____ _____

Rounded number _____ _____ _____ _____ _____

PROBLEM SOLVING
Logical Reasoning

At a school carnival, 5 students each write down a decimal. The student whose decimal is in the middle wins the grand prize, a colorful shirt. Kelvin's decimal is 3 tenths more than Ivan's. Sarah's decimal is 2 hundredths less than Ivan's. Bill's, which is 6.537, is 5 thousandths less than Kelvin's. If you rounded Ivan's number to the nearest tenth, that would be Joan's number. Which student wins the shirt?

 Read problems carefully to see what you know and what you have to find.

1. What person's number do you know for sure? _____

2. What is the number? _____

3. Knowing that number, whose number can you find next? _____

4. What is the number? _____

5. Using that number, what must be Ivan's number? _____

6. Whose numbers are left to find? _____

7. What are those numbers? _____

8. Order the five numbers from the least to the greatest.

Name _____ _____ _____ _____ _____

Number _____ _____ _____ _____ _____

9. Which student won the shirt? _____

Another game at the carnival involved a large drum. In the drum were all the decimals in the thousandths from 0.001 to 0.999. The student picking the greatest number won a year's supply of chalk and a chalkboard. Mary's number was 0.02 less than Ching's. Pedro's number was halfway between Mary's and Ching's. Florence's number was 0.005 greater than Sean's which was 0.07 more than Pedro's. Pedro's number was 0.583. Who won?

10. Whose number do you know for sure? _____

11. What is the number? _____

12. Order the other numbers to find the winner.

Name _____ _____ _____ _____ _____

Number _____ _____ _____ _____ _____

13. Who was the winner? _____

Add and Subtract Decimals/ Guess and Check

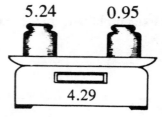

5.24   0.95

4.29

Estimate first. Then add or subtract.

		Estimate				**Estimate**
8.62	→	9				
0.7	→	1		5.24	→	5
+ 9.04	→	+ 9		− 0.95	→	− 1
18.36		19		4.29		4

Estimate first. Then find the missing weight.

1.   3.64   7.89

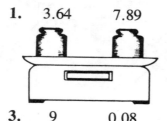

Estimate _____

Sum   _____

2.   7.5   13.69

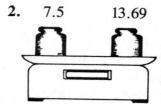

Estimate _____

Sum   _____

3.   9   0.08

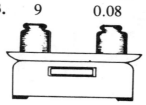

Estimate _____

Sum   _____

4.   3.2   0.69   5.85

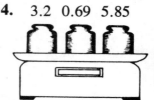

Estimate _____

Sum   _____

5. 17.68   ?

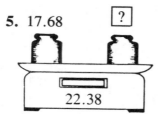

22.38

Estimate _____

Sum   _____

6.   ?   9.4

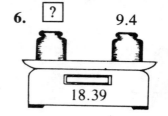

18.39

Estimate _____

Sum   _____

7.   6.3   ?   0.7

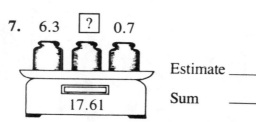

17.61

Estimate _____

Sum   _____

8. 4.67   7.8   ?

33

Estimate _____

Sum   _____

Use these three decimals. | 2.1 | | 5.7 | | 3.6 |

1. Write two addition sentences.

_____   _____

2. Write two subtraction sentences.

_____   _____

3. Explain how you knew which two decimals must be addends. _____

_____

Use these three decimals. | 7.37 | | 5.4 | | 1.97 |

4. Write two addition sentences.

_____   _____

5. Write two subtraction sentences.

_____   _____

6. Tell why it was possible to make two subtraction sentences using only
the three decimals shown.

_____

Complete the sentences.

  7. $7.12 + .04 = $ ____ , so ____ $ - 7.12 = 0.4$

  8. $1.56 + 7.3 = $ ____ , so ____ $ - 7.3 = 1.56$

  9. $9.6 - 2.8 = $ ____ , so ____ $ + 2.8 = 9.6$

10. $10.35 - 8.1 = $ ____ , so $8.1 + $ ____ $ = 10.35$

11. Find the missing decimal. Write two addition and two subtraction
sentences.

  | 19.2 | | 2.5 | | |

_____

12. How did you find the missing decimal? _____

STAMPS
1-ounce letter $.22
Postcard $.14

PROBLEM SOLVING
Guess and Check

Dan bought 5 stamps for $.94. Some of them were $.14. Some were $.22. How many of each type of stamp did Dan buy?

Guess A	Check
2 at $.22	2 × $.22 = $.44
3 at $.14	3 × $.14 = $.42
	Total = $.86

1. Is **Guess A** the correct combination of stamps? _____

2. Suppose you wanted to guess 4 at $.22 and 1 at $.14. Complete the chart below to show this.

 TIP

Use the results of your first guess and check to make a better guess.

Guess B	Check
_____ at $.22	_____ × $.22 = _____
_____ at $.14	_____ × $.14 = _____

3. What is the total amount of money spent in **Guess B**? _____

4. What is the difference between the total amount in **Guess B** and the amount of money Dan spent?

_____

5. What are the other possible guesses? _____

_____

6. Complete **Guess C** with new numbers. If this guess is not correct, try
again on another piece of paper.

Guess C	Check
_____ at $.22	_____ × $.22 = _____
_____ at $.14	_____ × $.14 = _____
	Total = _____

7. How many of each kind of stamp did Dan buy?_____

_____

 You may wish to use a calculator for this exercise.

8. Sara bought 14 stamps for $2.44. Some of them were $.22 and some
were $.14. How many of each type of stamp did she buy? Write your
guesses and checks on the chart.

	Guess	Check
A	_____ at $.22	_____ × $.22 = _____
	_____ at $.14	_____ × $.14 = _____
		Total = _____
B		
C		

Answer: _____

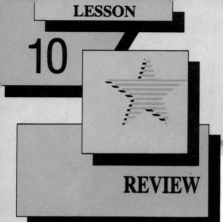

Multiply and Divide Decimals/ Multi-Step Problems

In a magic square the sum of each row, column, and diagonal is the same.

A

			22.5
6	4.5	12	
13.5	7.5	1.5	→22.5
3	10.5	9	

↓
22.5

B

			9
2.4	1.8	4.8	
5.4	3	0.6	→9
1.2	4.2	3.6	

↓
9

1. Multiply each member of magic square **A** by 0.3 to form a new square.

3. Divide each member of magic square **B** by 3 to form a new square.

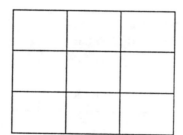

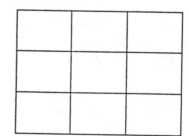

2. What is the new sum of each row, column, and diagonal?

_____

4. What is the new sum of each row, column, and diagonal?

_____

1. Place one of the digits in each box to form the greatest product.

2. What is the least product possible using the same 4 digits? _____

3. If you doubled both of the factors in either exercise 1 or exercise 2, how would it change the product? _____

4. Place one digit in each box to find a quotient of 0.43.

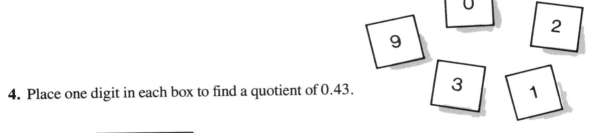

5. If you doubled both the dividend and the divisor in exercise 4, how would it change the quotient?

_____

PROBLEM SOLVING
Multi-Step Problems

When building the Erie Canal, a crew of 7 men could dig 24.5 feet per week. After working for 5 weeks, 2 of the men hurt their backs. The other men continued to work for 3 more weeks. How many feet of the canal were dug in all?

 Breaking a problem into parts makes it easier to solve.

1. How many feet could each man dig in 1 week?

_____

2. How many feet could 1 man dig in 8 weeks?

_____

3. How many feet could 1 man dig in 5 weeks?

_____

4. How many men worked for the full 8 weeks?

_____

5. What was the total distance dug by those men?

_____

6. How many men worked for only 5 weeks?

_____

7. What was the total amount dug by those men?

_____

You have made the problem simpler by breaking it into two parts.

8. One group of men worked for 8 weeks. They

dug _____ feet.

9. Another group of men worked for 5 weeks.

They dug _____ feet.

10. How many feet of the canal were dug in all? _____

Years later, near the canal site, 8 workers put in 2.4 miles of barbed-wire fence in 1 day. There were a total of 106.2 miles of fence to be put up. After working for 2 weeks, 6 days per week, 3 of the workers had to leave. How much longer did it take the remaining 5 workers to finish the job?

You may wish to use a calculator with these exercises.

11. How could you simplify the problem to make the solution easier?

_____

_____

_____

12. How much fence did the 8 workers put up? _____

13. How much fence did the 5 workers have to put up alone? _____

14. How much fence did the 5 workers put up in 1 week? _____

15. How long did it take to finish? _____

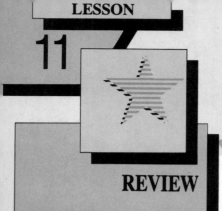

Factors and Multiples/ Look for a Pattern

Find two numbers in the number pile and write them next to their greatest common factor below. Use all the numbers from the pile only once.

1. 4 _____ _____

2. 12 _____ _____

3. 16 _____ _____

4. 20 _____ _____

5. Ring all multiples of 2. Put a square around all multiples of 3. Make a triangle around all multiples of 4.

1	2	3	4	5	6	7	8	9	10
11	12	13	14	15	16	17	18	19	20
21	22	23	24	25	26	27	28	29	30
31	32	33	34	35	36	37	38	39	40

6. What is the **least common multiple** of 2, 3, and 4?

_____

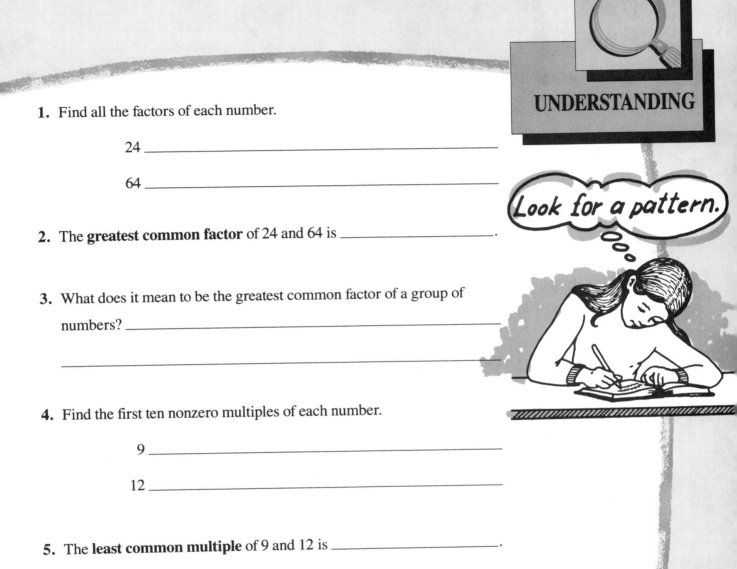

1. Find all the factors of each number.

24 _____

64 _____

Look for a pattern.

UNDERSTANDING

2. The **greatest common factor** of 24 and 64 is _____.

3. What does it mean to be the greatest common factor of a group of numbers? _____

_____

4. Find the first ten nonzero multiples of each number.

9 _____

12 _____

5. The **least common multiple** of 9 and 12 is _____.

6. What does it mean to be the least common multiple of a group of numbers? _____

_____

PROBLEM SOLVING
Look for a Pattern

General Ulysses S. Grant wanted more color on the uniforms of his troops. He selected one company to try out his ideas. He handed out new hats to every 16th person and new sashes to every 24th person. There were between 200 and 300 soldiers in the company and the last soldier received both a hat and a sash. How many soldiers were there in the company?

 TIP Making an organized list helps you to see patterns.

1. The soldiers lined up in a long row and numbered off. A hat was given to the 16th person in line and every 16th person after that. A sash was given to the 24th person and every 24th person after that. List the numbers of the first 5 soldiers who received hats and sashes.

   Soldiers receiving hats _____ _____ _____ _____ _____

   Soldiers receiving sashes _____ _____ _____ _____ _____

2. What was the number of the first soldier that received both a hat and a sash?

   _____

3. What would be the number of the next soldier who received both a hat and a sash? Continue the list you made in exercise 1 if you need to.

   _____

4. What is the pattern of the numbers of the soldiers who received both a hat and a sash?

   _____

5. How are 16, 24, and 48 related?

_____

_____

6. What are the soldiers' numbers between 200 and 300 that received both a hat and a sash?

_____

When marching into battle, General Lee liked his troops to be in either 16 rows or 18 rows. On one march less than 1,000 troops could form into either 16 or 18 rows, with an equal number in each row. What is the greatest number of troops possible?

 You may wish to use a calculator for these exercises.

7. Find the least number of troops that could be formed into 16 and 18 even rows.

_____

8. Develop a pattern of numbers which are divisible by both 16 and 18.

_____

9. What is the greatest number of troops possible? _____

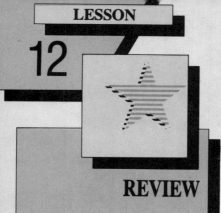

Mixed Numbers and Improper Fractions/Make a Model

A **fraction** or a **mixed number** tells what part of the shapes are shaded.

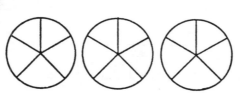

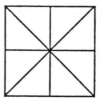

$\frac{5}{5} + \frac{5}{5} + \frac{3}{5} = \frac{13}{5}$ or $2\frac{3}{5}$ are shaded

$\frac{8}{8} + \frac{4}{8} = \frac{12}{8}$ or $1\frac{4}{8}$ or $1\frac{1}{2}$ are shaded

Write the fraction and mixed number, in lowest terms, that tell how much of each shape is shaded.

1.

fraction _____

mixed number _____

2.

fraction _____

mixed number _____

3.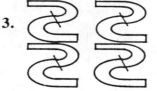

fraction _____

mixed number _____

4.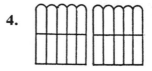

fraction _____

mixed number _____

Write the equivalent fraction or mixed number in lowest terms. Then draw in the parts of the given shapes.

5.
fraction $\frac{10}{3}$

mixed number _____

6.
fraction _____

mixed number $1\frac{3}{4}$

7.
fraction $\frac{12}{4}$

mixed number _____

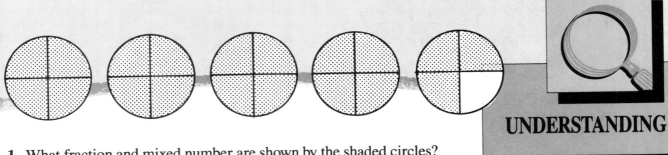

1. What fraction and mixed number are shown by the shaded circles?

fraction_____ mixed number_____

2. If 3 more shaded circles were added, what fraction would be shown?

fraction_____ mixed number_____

3. If the shaded circles were divided into eighths what fraction would be

shown? _____

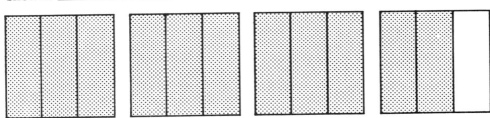

4. What fraction and mixed number are shown by the shaded squares?

fraction_____ mixed number_____

5. Add enough squares marked in thirds to bring the total to $\frac{17}{3}$.

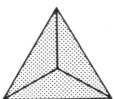 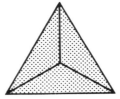 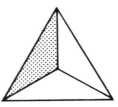

6. If you doubled the number of completely shaded triangles, what fraction and mixed number would be shown?

fraction_____ mixed number_____

PROBLEM SOLVING
Make a Model

At the first Thanksgiving the Pilgrims prepared many pies. They cut each pie into four pieces. After they served $6\frac{1}{2}$ pies it appeared they would run out, so they cut each piece of the remaining pies into 2 pieces. After $7\frac{1}{2}$ of these pies were eaten, they cut the pieces in 9 more pies in half again. When the feast was over there were 56 pieces left. How many pieces were eaten in all?

 Breaking a problem into parts and drawing a model of each part may help you find the solution.

1. How many pieces were eaten when the pies were in fourths? _____ Make a model to help you.

2. After the pieces were cut in halves, how many pieces were in each pie?

_____

3. How many pieces were in the $7\frac{1}{2}$ pies? _____

4. After the final cuts, how many pieces were in each pie? _____

5. How many pieces were in the 9 pies? _____

6. How many of those pieces were eaten? _____

7. How many pieces were eaten in all? _____

When measuring distance as a surveyor, Thomas Jefferson had his measuring stick divided into different measures. Each of the first 5 feet were marked off in $\frac{1}{2}$ ft units. The second 5 feet were marked off in $\frac{1}{4}$ ft units. The third 5 feet were marked in $\frac{1}{8}$ ft units. When he measured the width of a certain gate, he found that it measured 8 of the units from the first 5 feet, 20 of the units from the second 5 feet, and 36 from the third 5 feet. What was the width of the gate?

8. Make a model of what the measuring stick looked like.

9. List the 3 measures that made up the width of the gate.

_____   _____   _____

10. What was the width of the gate? _____

Add and Subtract Fractions/ Scale Drawing

Add $2\frac{1}{2} + 3\frac{5}{8} =$

$2\frac{4}{8} + 3\frac{5}{8} = 5\frac{9}{8}$

$= 6\frac{1}{8}$

Subtract $3\frac{1}{5} - 1\frac{3}{10} =$

$3\frac{2}{10} - 1\frac{3}{10} =$

$2\frac{12}{10} - 1\frac{3}{10} = 1\frac{9}{10}$

Use the number lines to help you answer the following questions.

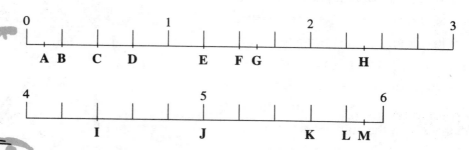

1. **A + F =** _____

2. **G + E =** _____

3. **M − I =** _____

4. **H − F =** _____

5. **I + L + K =** _____

6. **C + E − F =** _____

7. Add the number which is halfway between 4 and **I** to the number that is halfway between **K** and **L**.

8. How much greater is the number halfway between **E** and **F** than the number halfway between **B** and **C**?

_____ _____

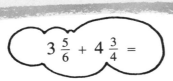

$$3\frac{5}{6} + 4\frac{3}{4} =$$

1. Do not add the two fractions above. Will the answer be between 7 and 8 or between 8 and 9?

_____

2. How did you find the answer? _____

_____

_____

_____

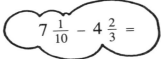

$$7\frac{1}{10} - 4\frac{2}{3} =$$

3. Do not subtract the two fractions above. Will the answer be between 3 and 4 or between 2 and 3?

_____

4. How do you know that? _____

_____

_____

_____

Without using your pencil, determine the whole number part of each answer.

5. $2\frac{3}{7} + 3\frac{1}{6} =$ _____   **6.** $8\frac{5}{7} - 6\frac{3}{8} =$ _____

7. $6\frac{3}{5} + 5\frac{4}{7} =$ _____   **8.** $9\frac{1}{3} - 4\frac{1}{2} =$ _____

PROBLEM SOLVING
Scale Drawing

When the Kelsons went to California in 1849, they carried along many maps to help them. The map below shows the route they used from Philadelphia to St. Louis.

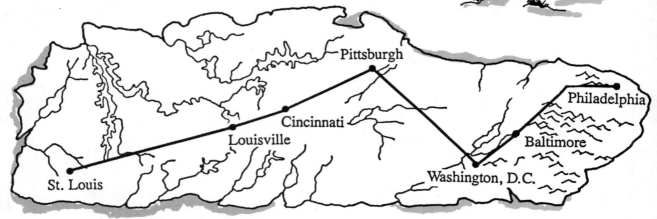

Each inch represents 200 miles.

 TIP Breaking a problem into smaller parts makes it easier to solve.

1. How far is it from Washington, D. C. to Pittsburgh in inches? _____

2. About how many miles would that be? _____

3. About how many miles did the Kelsons travel to Pittsburgh?

	Inches	Miles
a. Philadelphia to Baltimore	_____	_____
b. Baltimore to Washington, D. C.	_____	_____
c. Washington, D. C. to Pittsburgh	_____	_____
d. Totals	_____	_____

4. How many miles farther is it from Philadelphia to Cincinnati than from Cincinnati to St. Louis?

_____

5. Explain how you found the answer to exercise 4. _____

_____

When Lewis and Clark explored the West, they made maps of all their travels. We use some of those maps to this day. Below is a replica of one of those maps. How much farther is it from Ft. Mandan to Ft. Clatsap than from St. Louis to Ft. Mandan?

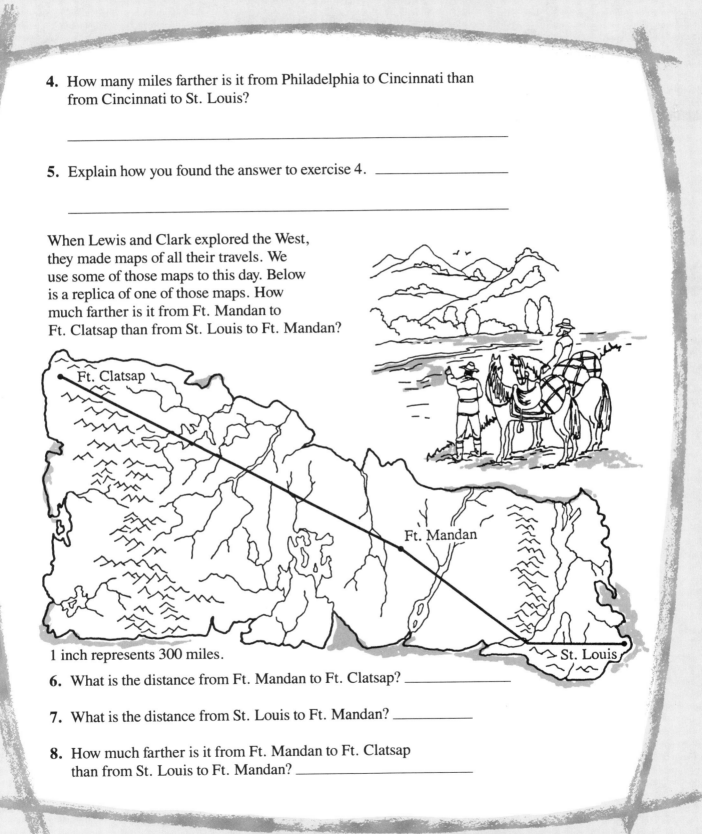

1 inch represents 300 miles.

6. What is the distance from Ft. Mandan to Ft. Clatsap? _____

7. What is the distance from St. Louis to Ft. Mandan? _____

8. How much farther is it from Ft. Mandan to Ft. Clatsap than from St. Louis to Ft. Mandan? _____

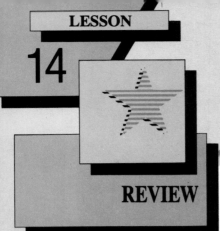

Multiply and Divide Fractions/ Work Backwards

Multiply: $\frac{4}{5} \times \frac{3}{8} =$

$\frac{4}{5} \times \frac{3}{8} =$

$\frac{12}{40} = \frac{3}{10}$

Divide: $\frac{5}{6} \div \frac{2}{3} =$

$\frac{5}{6} \times \frac{3}{2} =$

$\frac{15}{12} = 1\frac{1}{4}$

Look at the smaller figure. Multiply to find the value of the larger figure.

1.

2.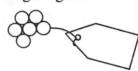

_____

3.

4.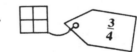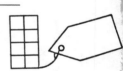

_____

5.

6.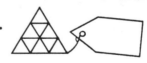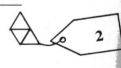

_____

Look at the larger figure. Divide to find the value of the smaller figure.

7.

8.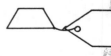

_____

$$6 \times \frac{2}{3} = 4$$

1. In this example, when 6 is multiplied by $\frac{2}{3}$ the answer is less than 6. When you multiply a whole number by a fraction less than 1, is the answer always less than the whole number? _____

_____

Try some other examples to see.

2. Multiply two fractions, both less than one. Is the answer greater than or less than either of the fractions being multiplied? _____

_____

Try some examples to see.

$$12 \div \frac{2}{3} = 18$$

3. In this example, when 12 is divided by $\frac{2}{3}$ the answer is greater than 12. When you divide a whole number by a fraction less than 1, is the answer always greater than the whole number? _____

_____

Try some examples to see.

4. Divide a fraction less than 1 by another fraction less than 1. Is the answer greater than or less than either of the fractions?

_____

Try some examples to see.

PROBLEM SOLVING
Work Backwards

Once there was a very wealthy man. He was also very stingy with his money. But, occasionally, he would give dimes to children. One day he started with a pocket full of dimes. He gave $\frac{1}{4}$ of his dimes to the first child he saw. Then he gave $\frac{1}{2}$ of what was left to a little girl. Finally, he gave the rest of the dimes, 9 in all, to a young schoolboy. How many dimes did the man start with?

 Checking your work as you go makes a correct solution more likely.

1. Since you know that the schoolboy received 9 dimes, start with that information and work backwards.

   Go back in the paragraph to before the man gave money to the little girl. Half of the money he had went to her. Where did the other half of the money go?

   _____

2. How many dimes did the little girl receive? _____

3. How many dimes did the man have before he gave some to the

   little girl? _____

4. Check yourself at this point.
   If the man gave half the dimes to the little girl, would he have 9 dimes

   left to give to the schoolboy? _____

5. Now go backwards in the story to the amount given to the first child. That child received $\frac{1}{4}$ of the original amount of dimes. What fraction of

   the original dimes are left after that? _____

6. If $\frac{3}{4}$ of the dimes is 18 dimes, how much is $\frac{1}{4}$ of the dimes?

_____

7. How many dimes did the wealthy man start with?

_____

Reread the story and see if your answer checks.

8. Would the last child receive 9 dimes? _____

One year the United States government spent its entire education budget on elementary schools. One third of the budget went to grades 2 and 3. One sixth of the rest went to grades 5 and 6. One half of what was left went to grade 4. The remaining amount, $15 million dollars, went to kindergartens and grade 1. What was the total budget for education that year?

9. Find the amount of money given to each grade level.

Grade 1 and kindergarten	$15 million
4th grade	_____
Total spent on K, 1st and 4th grades	_____
5th and 6th grades	_____
Total spent on K, 1st, 4th, 5th and 6th grades	_____
2nd and 3rd grades	_____

10. What was the total budget for education that year? _____
Check your solution by solving the problem with your answer.

Cumulative Review

DIRECTIONS
Read each question. Choose the best answer. Mark that answer in the space provided at the bottom of the page.

1 Rounded to tenths this number is 6.7.
Rounded to ones this number is 7.0.
The number is
a 7.73
b 6.76
c 6.66
d 6.47
e NH

2 Using the digits 5, 6, and 9, what is the greatest number you can make?
f 6.59
g 9.56
h 9.87
j 0.965
k NH

3 Which of the following numbers are all multiples of 3?
a 12, 36, 63
b 13, 23, 33
c 3, 4, 5
d 3, 6, 32
e NH

4 Which number has the factors 4, 8, 16, and 32?
f 4
g 8
h 16
j 32
k NH

5 What fraction is shown by the shaded region?

a $\frac{7}{2}$
b 15
c 3
d $4\frac{1}{2}$
e NH

6 If you shaded in 2 more parts, what fraction would be shown?

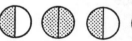

f $\frac{9}{3}$
g $4\frac{1}{2}$
h $\frac{7}{4}$
j $2\frac{1}{4}$
k NH

1 ⓐ ⓑ ⓒ ⓓ ⓔ
2 ⓕ ⓖ ⓗ ⓙ ⓚ
3 ⓐ ⓑ ⓒ ⓓ ⓔ

4 ⓕ ⓖ ⓗ ⓙ ⓚ
5 ⓐ ⓑ ⓒ ⓓ ⓔ
6 ⓕ ⓖ ⓗ ⓙ ⓚ

7 Which of these numbers all can be rounded to 9.2?
   a   9.15, 9.23, 9.27
   b   9.18, 9.17, 9.11
   c   9.23, 9.28, 9.22
   d   9.17, 9.18, 9.21

8 Which of these numbers are in order from least to greatest?
   f   1.23, 1.4, 1.53, 1.8
   g   3.45, 3.39, 3.78, 4.56
   h   6.08, 6.80, 6.88, 6.68
   j   7.7, 7.07, 7.77, 7.70

9 If you doubled both of the factors in the problem below, what would be the new product?

$$\begin{array}{r} 3.4 \\ \times\ 6.7 \\ \hline \end{array}$$

   a   11.39
   b   22.78
   c   45.56
   d   91.12

10 What is the greatest common factor of 6 and 8?
   f   48
   g   8
   h   24
   j   2

11 What is the least common multiple of 4 and 10?
   a   40
   b   20
   c   4
   d   2

12 If you doubled the number of shaded triangles, what fraction would be shown?

   f $4\frac{1}{3}$
   g $7\frac{1}{3}$
   h $6\frac{4}{6}$
   j $\frac{11}{6}$

7 ⓐ ⓑ ⓒ ⓓ
8 ⓕ ⓖ ⓗ ⓙ
9 ⓐ ⓑ ⓒ ⓓ

10 ⓕ ⓖ ⓗ ⓙ
11 ⓐ ⓑ ⓒ ⓓ
12 ⓕ ⓖ ⓗ ⓙ

13 Bryan's number is 6 tenths larger than Maria's, whose is twice as large as Joe's, whose is 3 tenths less than Gina's, whose is 4.5. Bryan's number is:

a 4.2
b 4.5
c 8.4
d 9.0

14 Eight animals, some chickens and some pigs, were in a field. There were a total of 22 legs. How many pigs were there?

f 3
g 5
h 4
j 6

15 If 8 men can paint a house in 14.4 hours, how long will it take one man to paint it?

a 1.4 hours
b 7.2 hours
c 28.8 hours
d 115.2 hours

16 A group of 12 tricycles and bicycles were in the window of the sport shop. They had a total of 33 wheels. How many tricycles were there?

f 3
g 9
h 6
j 12

17 What number between 400 and 500 is divisible by both 6 and 8?

a 440
b 460
c 480
d 490

18 What is the largest 3-digit number divisible by both 12 and 30?

f 998
g 960
h 956
j 942

13 (a) (b) (c) (d)
14 (f) (g) (h) (j)
15 (a) (b) (c) (d)

16 (f) (g) (h) (j)
17 (a) (b) (c) (d)
18 (f) (g) (h) (j)

19 Rex put some chairs in rows. When he made 5 equal rows, he had 1 left over. When he made 4 equal rows, he had 1 left over. Finally, he made 9 equal rows and had none left over. How many chairs are there if he had fewer than 100?

   a 56
   b 61
   c 81
   d 96

20 At a party, a total of 65 slices of oranges were eaten. Some of the oranges had 6 slices and some had 7. If 4 slices were left, how many whole oranges were there?

   f 7 oranges cut into 7 slices and 6 oranges cut into 6 slices
   g 7 oranges cut into 7 slices and 3 oranges cut into 6 slices
   h 9 oranges cut into 7 slices and 3 oranges cut into 6 slices
   j 9 oranges cut into 7 slices and 1 orange cut into 6 slices

21 Lloyd gave $\frac{1}{4}$ of his grapes to Lea. Then he gave $\frac{1}{2}$ of what was left to Lynn. Lloyd ended up with 9 pieces, which he fed his dog. How many pieces did he start with?

   a 72
   b 54
   c 45
   d 24

22 Steph spent half her money at the movies. Then she spent half of what she had left at the card shop. She had 15¢ left. How much money did Steph have at the start?

   f 30¢
   g 45¢
   h 60¢
   j 90¢

23 Harold spent $\frac{1}{3}$ of his money on a watch for his mother. Then he spent $5.00 for a pen and pencil set. He spent $\frac{1}{2}$ of what was left on a belt. If he ended up with $3.50, how much did he start with?

   a $24
   b $20
   c $18
   d $15

19 ⓐ ⓑ ⓒ ⓓ
20 ⓕ ⓖ ⓗ ⓙ

21 ⓐ ⓑ ⓒ ⓓ
22 ⓕ ⓖ ⓗ ⓙ
23 ⓐ ⓑ ⓒ ⓓ

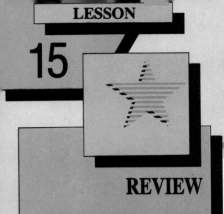

Decimals and Fractions/
Logical Reasoning

This shaded area is equal to $\frac{2}{10}$ or 0.2.

Find the fraction and decimal for each of these shaded areas.

1.

fraction _____

decimal _____

2.

fraction _____

decimal _____

3.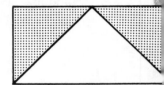

fraction _____

decimal _____

4.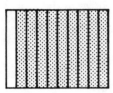

fraction _____

decimal _____

5.

fraction _____

decimal _____

6.

fraction _____

decimal _____

Estimate the decimal or fraction for each of these.

7.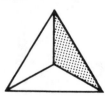

fraction _____

8.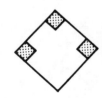

decimal _____

9.

fraction _____

decimal _____

Estimate to find the range.

A		B		C		D		E		F		G		H

0       $\frac{1}{4}$ $\frac{1}{2}$ $\frac{3}{4}$ 1

Where are these decimals located?

1. 0.4 _____   **2.** 0.9 _____   **3.** 0.2 _____   **4.** 0.7 _____

5. 0.11 _____   **6.** 0.76 _____   **7.** 0.48 _____   **8.** 0.23 _____

A		B		C		D		E		F		G		H		I		J

0   0.1   0.2   0.3   0.4   0.5   0.6   0.7   0.8   0.9   1

Where are these fractions located?

9. $\frac{1}{3}$ _____   **10.** $\frac{3}{4}$ _____   **11.** $\frac{5}{8}$ _____   **12.** $\frac{12}{13}$ _____

0   A   B   C   D   E   F   1

Decide which letter best represents each fraction or decimal.

13. $\frac{1}{2}$ _____   **14.** 0.07 _____   **15.** 0.7 _____

16. $\frac{2}{3}$ _____   **17.** 0.33 _____   **18.** $\frac{11}{12}$ _____

A fifth grade teacher made up 18 cards containing fractions and 18 cards containing decimals. She put 12 fraction cards in one box, 12 decimal cards in another box, and 6 of each kind in a third box. She labeled one box "fractions," another "decimals," and a third "mixed." None of the labels matched the contents of the box. By selecting one card from any box, how could you correctly identify the contents of each box?

$$\frac{1}{2} \quad \frac{1}{4} \quad \frac{3}{4} \quad \begin{array}{l} 0.91 \\ 3.062 \end{array}$$

Identifying all possible cases can lead to a solution.

1. What type of cards could be in the box marked "fractions"?

_____

2. How do you know that? _____

_____

_____

3. Could you be sure of the contents of this box if you picked a card from it?

_____

4. What type of cards could be in the box marked "decimals"?

_____

5. Could you be sure of the contents of that box if you picked a card from it?

_____

6. What type of cards could be in the box marked "mixed"?

_____

7. Could you be sure of the contents of this box is you picked a card from it?

_____

8. Assume you draw a fraction card from the "mixed" box.

What are the contents of each box? _____

_____

_____

Of the 12 mixed cards, 3 of the fractions on the cards are equivalent to $\frac{1}{2}$ and 3 of the fractions on the cards are equivalent to $\frac{1}{3}$. Three of the decimals on the cards are equal to 0.3 and the other 3 decimals are equal to 0.7. How many cards do you have to draw from the box to make sure that you have two cards which name the same number?

List possible draws in order. Try to avoid making a match as long as possible.

9. How many cards must you draw to make sure you have two matching cards?

_____

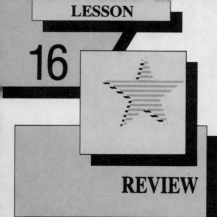
Percent/
Use Circle Graphs

Percent means per hundred.
Percent is used to compare a number to 100.

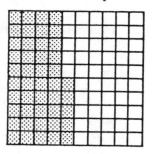

45 squares are shaded.

$\frac{45}{100}$ is shaded.

0.45 is shaded.
45% is shaded.

Find the percent.

1.

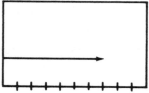

What percent of the field has the
team covered?

_____

2.

What percent of a dollar is shown?

_____

3.

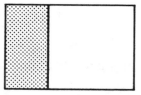

What percent of the wall is painted?

_____

4.

What percent of the shapes are
triangles?

_____

5.

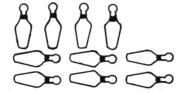

What percent of the pins are down?

_____

6.

What percent of the cube is shown?

_____

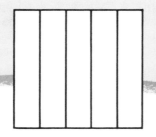

1. Shade in 40% of this square.

2. How did you find 40%? _____

_____

_____

3. What percent is not shaded? _____

4. How do you know that? _____

_____

5. If you shaded in twice as much as you did, what percent would be

shaded? _____

6. Then what percent would not be shaded? _____

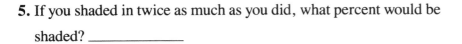

7. Shade in 75% of this circle.

8. How did you find 75%? _____

_____

9. What percent is not shaded? _____

10. Make a circle drawing that is 175% shaded.

PROBLEM SOLVING
Circle Graphs

Henri and Sean surveyed the students in their school to find out their favorite school lunches. They graphed the results on this circle graph.

1. About what percent of the students surveyed preferred pizza?

_____

2. If a total of 300 students were asked, how many picked pizza as their favorite lunch?

_____

3. How did you find your answer?

_____

_____

FAVORITE SCHOOL LUNCHES

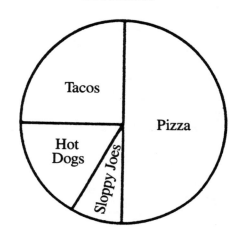

4. About what percent of the students surveyed preferred Sloppy Joes?

_____

5. How did you find that percentage? _____

_____

6. If 300 students were surveyed, how many preferred Sloppy Joes?

_____

7. How did you find that answer? _____

_____

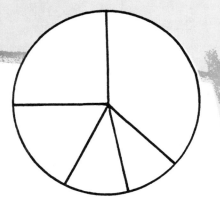

A circle graph can help you solve problems with percent.

The following are the results of asking 100 students what they do after school. Show the results on a circle graph.

Watch TV	|||| |||| |||| |||| |||| |||| ||||
Play	|||| |||| |||| |||| ||||
Do chores	|||| |||| |||| ||||
Do homework	|||| |||| |||
Take a nap	|||| ||

8. How did you decide how much of the circle should stand for the number of children that watched TV?

_____

_____

9. How did you decide how much of the circle should stand for the number of children that did chores?

_____

_____

10. If you asked a total of 300 children the same question, would you expect the circle graph showing their answers to change much?

_____

11. Why or why not? _____

_____

12. If the answers of the 300 children were similar to those of the 100 children, how many would

a. watch TV? _____ **b.** play? _____

c. do chores? _____ **d.** do homework? _____

e. take a nap? _____

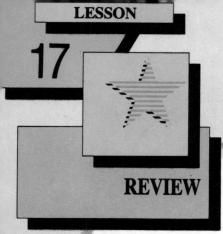

Metric Measurement/
Multi-Step Problems

In the metric system, there are three basic units of measure.

METER	**LITER**	**GRAM**
Measures length	Measures capacity	Measures mass
1 m = 100 cm	1L = 1,000 mL	1kg = 1,000 g

Use what you know about the metric system to match each picture with its proper metric measure.

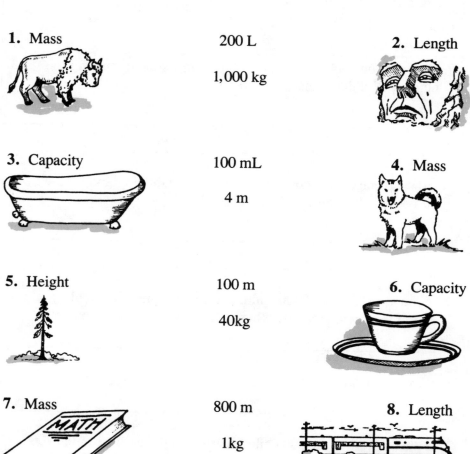

1. Mass

200 L

1,000 kg

2. Length

3. Capacity

100 mL

4 m

4. Mass

5. Height

100 m

40kg

6. Capacity

7. Mass

800 m

1kg

8. Length

1. What would you guess to be the mass of 12 dimes? _____

2. What would be the mass of 6 dimes? _____

3. Explain how you made your estimate. _____

_____

_____

4. How many meters would you guess the 3 cars to be? _____

5. How long would 2 cars be? _____

6. Explain how you made your estimate. _____

_____

_____

7. How many liters would you guess the 8 trash cans hold? _____

8. How many liters would 40 trash cans hold? _____

9. Explain how you made your estimate. _____

_____

_____

PROBLEM SOLVING
Multi-Step Problems

A bag with 10 marbles has a mass of 66 grams. The same bag with 20 marbles has a mass of 80 grams. What is the mass of the bag?

 TIP Sometimes you must use the information in a problem to find other information you need for the solution.

1. List the information you know.

_____

_____

_____

2. If you doubled the amounts you wrote for exercise 1, how would it read? _____

_____

_____

3. What other information can you find by putting together the statement from exercise 2 with the fact that one bag with 20 marbles has a mass of 80 grams?

_____

_____

4. How can you use this information to help you answer the original question?

_____

_____

5. What is the mass of the bag? _____

Thomas used 2 jars and 2 bowls to measure milk. He found that 2 jars and 1 bowl held a total of 4.8 liters. He also found that 2 bowls and 1 jar held a total of 4.2 liters. How much milk did 1 jar hold?

6. What information do you know from the paragraph?

_____

_____

_____

7. What other information can you find to help with the solution? _____

_____

_____

8. Use that information to find out how much milk the jar holds. Show your work here.

Customary Measurement/ Work Backwards

Length is measured in inches, feet, yards, and miles.
Weight is measured in ounces, pounds, and tons.
Capacity is measured in cups, pints, quarts, and gallons.

Ring the measure in each box that is **not equal** to the other two.

1.		2.		3.		4.	
D	2 qt	R	36 in.	M	48 oz	T	5,280 ft
E	1 gal	S	2 ft	N	3 lb	U	1,760 yd
F	4 pt	T	24 in.	O	36 oz	V	1,780 yd

5.		6.		7.		8.	
P	32 c	Q	3 tons	X	108 in.	S	24 pt
Q	4 qt	R	6,000 lb	Y	8 ft	T	3 gals
R	1 gal	S	3,000 lb	Z	3 yd	U	6 qt

9.		10.		11.		12.	
U	5 yd	C	$2\frac{1}{2}$ gal	M	$3\frac{1}{2}$ gal	A	6,000 lb
V	10 ft	D	40 oz	N	16 qt	B	2 tons
W	120 in.	E	34 oz	O	32 pt	C	64,000 oz

Write the letter of the ringed measure on the line above the box number.

$\overline{}$ $\overline{}$ $\overline{}$ $\overline{}$ $\overline{}$ $\overline{}$ $\overline{}$ $\overline{}$ $\overline{}$ $\overline{}$ $\overline{}$ $\overline{}$

 7   3   8   11 1 12 6 9 2 10   4 5

1. How much short of a yard is this? _____

2. How long would 4 of these sticks and 6 more inches be in yards

   and inches? _____

3. What would be the length from exercise 2, in feet and inches?

   _____

4. How would you balance 6 ounces using these weights?

   _____

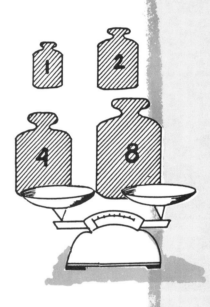

5. How would you balance 13 ounces using these weights?

   _____

6. Which of the weights from 1 to 15 ounces can you balance

   using these weights? _____

7. How do you know? _____

   _____

8. How many of these cups would it take to fill a gallon container?

   _____

9. How did you decide on your answer? _____

   _____

PROBLEM SOLVING
Work Backwards

At a mission during the Great Depression, peanuts were handed out to the needy. Mr. Hokomoto would give a scoop of peanuts to each person. Mrs. Hokomoto thought the scoop held 3 cups. One day she received a large barrel of peanuts. She counted every scoop as she emptied the barrel and decided that it held 48 gallons. When she turned the barrel over, it was marked "40 gallons." How many cups did each scoop actually hold?

When working with measures be sure they are all in the same unit.

1. How many cups are in a gallon? _____

2. How many cups are in 48 gallons? _____

3. How many scoops did Mrs. Hokomoto count? _____

4. How did you find the number of scoops? _____

   _____

   _____

5. Did each scoop hold more or less than 3 cups? _____

6. How do you know? _____

   _____

   _____

   _____

7. How many cups did the scoop actually hold? (16 × 40 = 640)

_____

When measuring a classmate at West Point, Douglas reported the height at 6 feet 7 inches. But this cadet was shorter than Douglas, who was only slightly over 6 feet tall. The other cadet later reported that he was exactly 5 feet 9 inches tall. Douglas then noticed that as a prank someone had cut off part of his 12 inch ruler. How many inches had they cut off?

8. Why did Douglas think that his classmate was 6 feet 7 inches tall?

_____

_____

9. How many lengths of his ruler did Douglas use to measure his

classmate? _____

10. How many inches is the classmate's actual height?

_____

11. What was the length of Douglas' ruler if he recorded the

height as 6 feet 7 inches? _____

Polygons, Lines and Angles/ Look for a Pattern

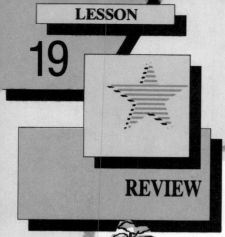

REVIEW

Polygons are closed, plane figures whose sides are made up of straight line segments.

 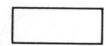 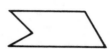

Lines and line segments are related, as are rays and angles.

  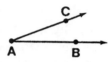

Fill in the chart with the correct name from the list at the right.

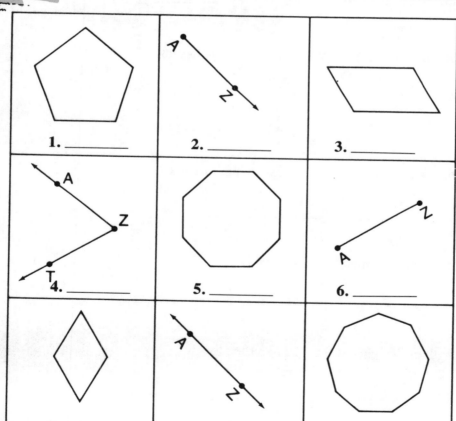

1. _____

2. _____

3. _____

4. _____

5. _____

6. _____

7. _____

8. _____

9. _____

nonagon

pentagon

$\xrightarrow{\;\bullet\;} \overline{AZ}$

$\overline{AZ}$

decagon

$\xleftrightarrow{\;} \overline{AZ}$

octagon

rhombus

parallelogram

$\angle$ **AZT**

ZAT

1. List all the different line segments in this diagram.

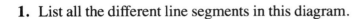

M   N   O   P   Q

2. List all the different angles in this diagram.

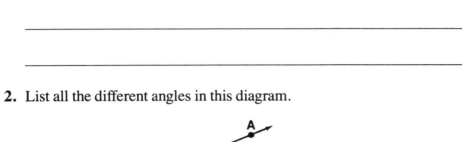

3. List all the triangles and all the parallelograms in this diagram.

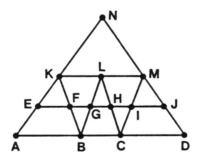

Triangles _____

_____

Parallelograms _____

_____

Eight Cherokee villages are connected by trails. There is a trail connecting each village with every other village. How many trails are there in all?

 Simplifying the problem often helps you find the solution.

1. If there were only 2 villages, how many trails would there be?

_____

2. If there were 3 villages, how many trails would there be?

_____

3. Find the number of trails for 4 and 5 villages and write them in the table.

Number of villages	Number of trails
1	_____
2	_____
3	_____
4	_____
5	_____

4. Look at the table and find a pattern. How many trails would there be for 6 villages?

_____

5. Continuing the pattern, how many trails would there be for 7 villages?

_____

6. For the 8 Cherokee Indian villages, how many trails are there

in all? _____

To encourage settlers in some areas of
the country, the United States government
divided up land into sections and then gave
away the land. In one area the land was
divided into squares 1 mile on a side.
Each settler could receive a rectangular
piece 1 mile by 2 miles. In how many
different ways could a 1 mile by 2 mile
rectangle be marked off in an area 8 miles
by 8 miles?

In a 3 mile by 3 mile square area there could be a total of 12 pieces
each 1 mile by 2 miles.

7. Set up a table listing the number of rectangles in squares of increasing
sizes. Look for a pattern.

Square	Number of Rectangles
1 × 1	0
2 × 2	_____
3 × 3	12
4 × 4	_____
5 × 5	_____
6 × 6	_____
7 × 7	_____

8. How many rectangles are there in an area 8 miles by 8 miles?

_____

Similar and Congruent Figures/
Solve a Simpler Problem

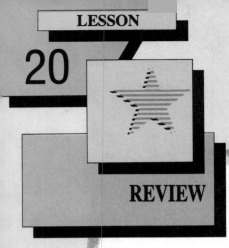

Congruent figures have exactly the same size and shape.

Similar figures have the same shape but not necessarily the same size.

 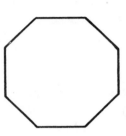 

Use the dot paper to draw a figure that is congruent to each figure shown.

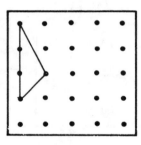 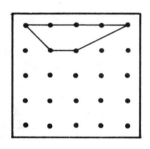 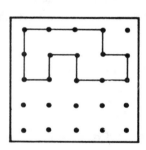 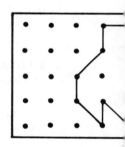

Use the dot paper to draw a figure that is similar to each figure shown.
Make the new figure larger than the original.

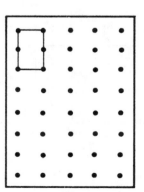 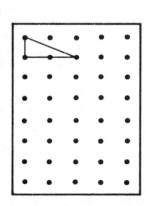 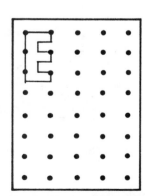 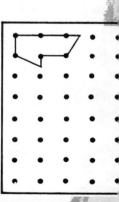

Show the lengths of the unknown sides for each of these congruent figures.

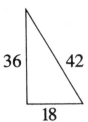

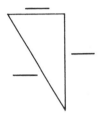

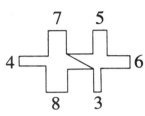

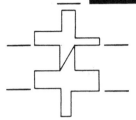

36   42

18

7   5

4   6

8   3

Show the lengths of the unknown sides for each of these similar figures.

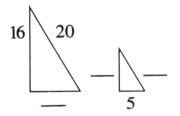

16   20

5

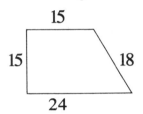

15

15   18

24

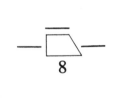

8

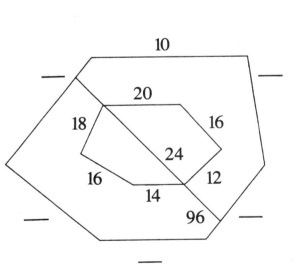

10

20

18   16

24

16   12

14

96

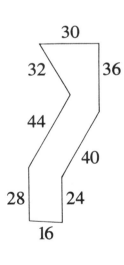

30

32   36

44

40

28   24

16

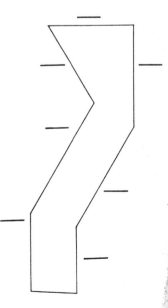

PROBLEM SOLVING
Solve a Simpler Problem

When traveling to Kentucky in 1827, Daniel Boone came to a flooded river. Before he could cross he needed to find out how wide the river was. He sighted the large tree from point **A** and drew a line on the ground from the river bank to **A.** Then he walked 18 paces from **A** to **B** and sighted the tree again. If the distance from **A** to **C** is 3 paces and the distance from **C** to the bank is 5 paces, how far is it across the river?

 Making a diagram helps in solving problems.

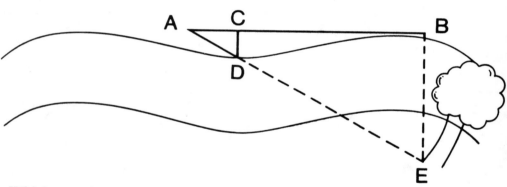

1. Which two triangles are similar? _____

2. How do you know that? _____

   _____

   _____

3. Which side in the large triangle compares to side **AC** in the small one?

   _____

4. Which side in the large triangle compares to side **CD** in the small one?

   _____

5. A side of the large triangle is how many times as long as a side

of the small triangle? _____

6. How far is it across the river? _____

7. Do you think this is an exact answer? _____

8. Why or why not? _____

_____

_____

On a mountain-climbing trip to Yosemite in 1905, Theodore Roosevelt came to a sheer rock wall. His guide told him that the cliff was 300 feet tall. Show how he could estimate the height by using similar triangles and making simple measurements. Place measurements in the diagram below which would show that the cliff is indeed 300 feet tall.

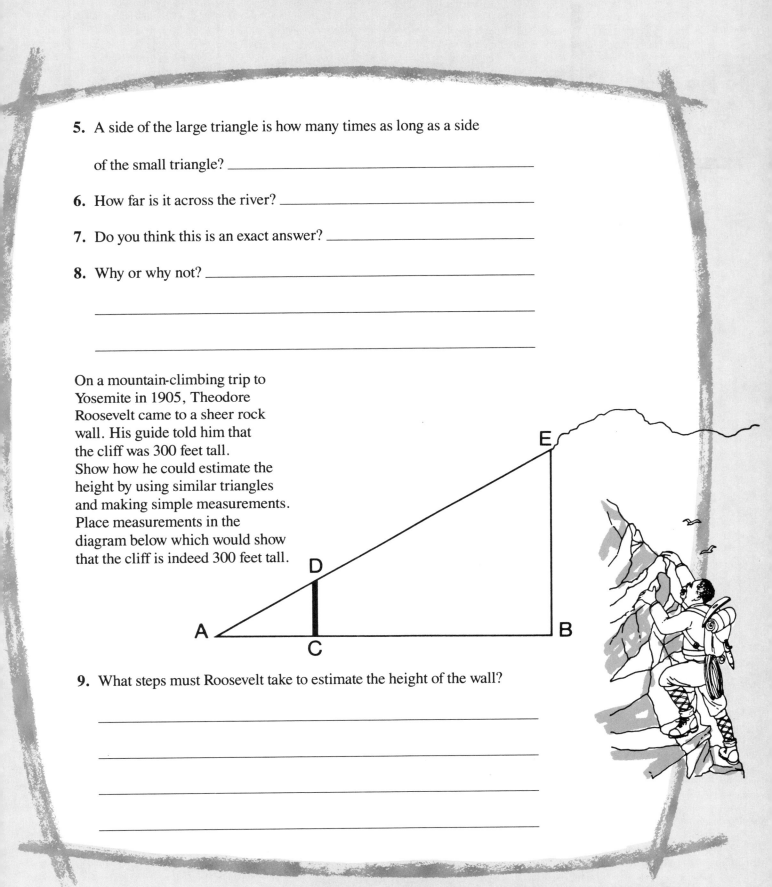

9. What steps must Roosevelt take to estimate the height of the wall?

_____

_____

_____

_____

Cumulative Review

DIRECTIONS

Read each question. Choose the best answer. Mark that answer in the space provided at the bottom of the page.

1 What fraction of this circle is shaded?

A $\frac{3}{4}$

B $\frac{2}{3}$

C $\frac{1}{3}$

D $\frac{1}{4}$

E None of these

2 The percent shown by this shaded area is:

F 12%

G 23%

H 45%

J 67%

K None of these

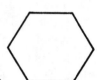

3 Which of these measures is closest to the height of a tall person?

A 1.8km

B 1.8m

C 1.8cm

D 1.8kg

E None of these

4 Which one of these measures is different from the other three?

F 160,400 inches

G 15,480 feet

H 5,280 yards

J 3 miles

K None of these

5 The correct name for this figure is a:

A quadrilateral

B pentagon

C hexagon

D octagon

E None of these

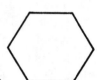

6 How would you classify these two shapes?

F They are congruent and similar.

G They are congruent but not similar.

H They are similar but not congruent.

J They are neither similar nor congruent.

K None of these

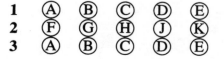

1 Ⓐ Ⓑ Ⓒ Ⓓ Ⓔ   4 Ⓕ Ⓖ Ⓗ Ⓙ Ⓚ
2 Ⓕ Ⓖ Ⓗ Ⓙ Ⓚ   5 Ⓐ Ⓑ Ⓒ Ⓓ Ⓔ
3 Ⓐ Ⓑ Ⓒ Ⓓ Ⓔ   6 Ⓕ Ⓖ Ⓗ Ⓙ Ⓚ

7 In which region is 0.53 located?

A A

B B

C C

D D

8 Which of the following best shows 67%?

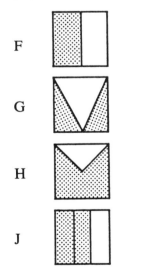

F

G

H

J

9 Jasmine used the ruler below to measure the length of the chalk tray. If she needed 6 lengths of this ruler and 5 more inches, how long was the chalk tray?

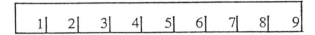

A Six feet five inches
B Sixty-five inches
C Fifty-nine inches
D Fifty-four inches

10 The two triangles below are similar. What is the length of the unknown side?

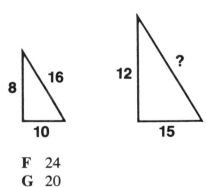

F 24
G 20
H 18
J 12

7 Ⓐ Ⓑ Ⓒ Ⓓ
8 Ⓕ Ⓖ Ⓗ Ⓙ

9 Ⓐ Ⓑ Ⓒ Ⓓ
10 Ⓕ Ⓖ Ⓗ Ⓙ

11 Five pairs of equivalent fractions are put on 10 cards. If Gina draws the cards one at a time, what is the greatest number of cards she could draw without selecting 2 cards containing equivalent fractions?

 A 3
 B 4
 C 6
 D 8

12 A drawer contains 12 identical red socks and 12 identical black socks. Mr. Harkin reached in and grabbed some socks without looking. What is the least number of socks he could have grabbed to be sure he has a matched pair?

 F 2
 G 3
 H 6
 J 13

13 If a 5 ft tall boy casts a shadow of 7 ft, how tall is a tree that casts a shadow of 84 ft?

 A 92 ft
 B 70 ft
 C 65 ft
 D 60 ft

Use the graph below for questions 14 and 15.

SUMMER WEATHER IN JESTI

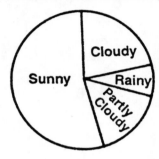

14 What percent of the days are cloudy

 F 10%
 G 20%
 H 27%
 J 32%

15 What percent of the days are not su

 A 60%
 B 50%
 C 40%
 D 30%

11 Ⓐ Ⓑ Ⓒ Ⓓ
12 Ⓕ Ⓖ Ⓗ Ⓙ
13 Ⓐ Ⓑ Ⓒ Ⓓ

14 Ⓕ Ⓖ Ⓗ Ⓙ
15 Ⓐ Ⓑ Ⓒ Ⓓ

16 When Larry stepped on the scale, it read 140 lbs. He knew he weighed more than that. He placed a 50 lb bag of salt on the scale and it read 40 lbs. How much did Larry actually weigh?

A 145 lbs
B 150 lbs
C 160 lbs
D 175 lbs

17 Marty broke a yard stick into 2 pieces. The short piece was exactly half as long as the longer piece. He measured his carpet with both pieces and found it was 3 long pieces and 6 short pieces wide. How wide was the carpet?

F 3 yards
G 4 yards
H 6 yards
J 9 yards

18 A 4-sided figure has 2 diagonals. A 5-sided figure has 5 diagonals. A 6-sided figure has 9 diagonals. How many diagonals are there in a 10-sided figure?

A 14
B 27
C 35
D 50

19 Kit walked 200 paces east and then 150 paces north. It took 250 paces to walk directly back to where he started. If he walked 120 paces east and 90 paces north, how many paces would he need to walk to return to the starting point?

F 200 paces
G 180 paces
H 160 paces
J 150 paces

16 Ⓐ Ⓑ Ⓒ Ⓓ
17 Ⓕ Ⓖ Ⓗ Ⓙ

18 Ⓐ Ⓑ Ⓒ Ⓓ
19 Ⓕ Ⓖ Ⓗ Ⓙ

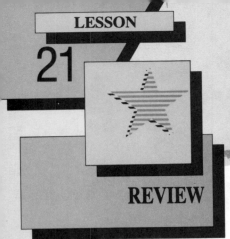

Perimeter and Area/ Make a Model

Perimeter is the distance around a figure.
Area is the number of square units it takes to cover a region.

Perimeter = 6 + 2 + 6 + 2 = 16 units

Area = 2 × 6 = 12 square units

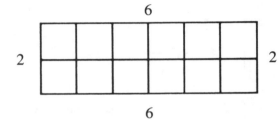

Connect the letters in order. Connect the last letter to **A.**

Find the perimeter and the area of each figure.

1.

Perimeter _____

Area _____

2.

Perimeter _____

Area _____

3.

Perimeter _____

Area _____

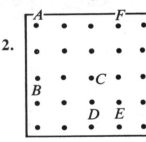

4.

Perimeter _____

Area _____

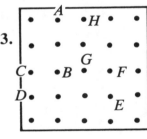

5.

Perimeter _____

Area _____

6.

Perimeter _____

Area _____

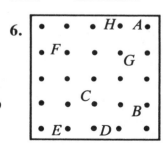

1. Draw a rectangle with an area of 6 square units.

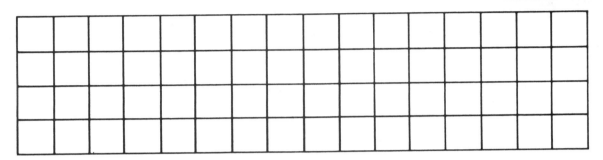

2. Draw a triangle with an area of 8 square units.

3. How did you find the lengths of the sides of this triangle?

_____

_____

4. Draw a rectangle with an area of 24 square units and a perimeter of 22 units.

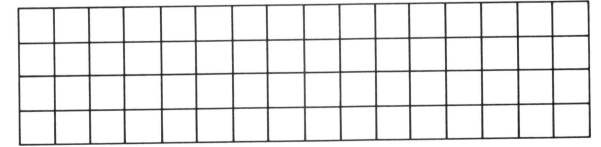

5. Explain how you drew the correct rectangle.

_____

_____

6. Now draw a rectangle with an area of 20 square units and a perimeter of 18 units.

The entrance to the White House is in the shape of a rectangle 5m by 3m. It is tiled with squares each 25cm on a side. How many squares were needed to tile the entrance?

A partial diagram is often enough to help find a solution.

1. Draw a rectangle and label the length and width as described in the paragraph.

2. How many squares 25cm long would fit along the length of the rectangle? Sketch a few in the diagram to help you find the answer.

_____

3. How many squares 25cm long fit along the width of the rectangle?

_____

4. What would be the total number of square tiles in the entrance?

_____

In the Rose Garden of the White House, a certain section needed to be resodded. Each piece of sod was 4 ft long and 2 ft wide. Five hundred pieces of sod were used. If the area was 80 ft long, how wide was it?

5. Draw a diagram of the area to be resodded. Do not label the width.

6. Sketch in a few of the pieces of sod along the length and the width.

7. Find the number of pieces that would fit along the length.

_____

8. How many pieces would fit along the width? _____

9. How wide is the area? _____

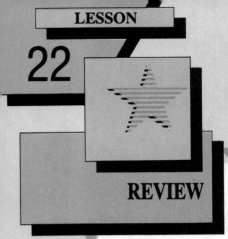
Volume/ Multi-Step Problems

Volume is a measure of capacity. It is the number of cubic units needed to fill a figure. Find the volume of these figures.

1.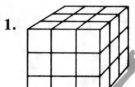

2.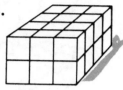

3.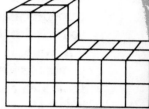

Volume = _____   Volume = _____   Volume = _____

Draw rectangular prisms with the volumes shown.

4. 6 cubic units   **5.** 20 cubic units   **6.** 36 cubic units

7. Draw three different rectangular prisms which have a volume of 24 cubic units.

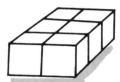

1. What are the dimensions of the rectangular prism above?

_____

2. What is the volume? _____

3. Make a sketch of a rectangular prism with dimensions twice those of the one pictured. Draw it next to the one pictured.

4. How does the volume of the new prism compare with the original one?

_____

5. Explain why this is true. _____

_____

_____

6. What would be the volume of a prism with a length the same as the smaller one above, a width 3 times as great, and a height that is twice as much?

_____

7. Describe what happens to the volume of a rectangular prism when one or more of the dimensions is increased by a multiple.

_____

_____

_____

PROBLEM SOLVING
Multi-Step Problems

To protect crates containing breakable items, the Pilgrims stacked them inside a rectangular prism formed by all their crates. If the final rectangular prism was 8 crates long, 5 crates wide, and 4 crates high, how many crates contained breakable items?

 **TIP** Making a diagram helps you to see the problem more clearly.

1. Make a sketch of the rectangular prism described.

2. What shape do the crates containing breakable items form?

_____

3. What is the length of the rectangular prism containing the crates with

breakable items? _____

4. How does that compare to the length of the large rectangular prism?

_____

5. What is the width of the shape containing the crates with

breakable items? _____

6. How does that compare to the width of the large rectangular prism?

_____

7. How will the heights compare? _____

8. What is the height of the crates with breakable items? _____

9. How many crates contain breakable items? _____

At the St. Louis World's Fair in the early 1900s an interesting contest was held. A dollar bill had been glued to each face of many cubes. The cubes were then stacked to form an $8 \times 8 \times 8$ cube. The grand prize was given to the first person who could figure out how many more dollar bills were glued to cubes on the outside of the large cube than were glued to cubes on the inside of the cube. Can you?

10. How many faces are on a cube? _____

11. What is the total number of faces on all the cubes? _____

12. Draw a sketch of the large cube.

13. How many cubes are "inside" the large cube? _____

14. Find the difference between the number of dollar bills on cubes on the inside and the number of dollar bills on cubes on the outside.

_____

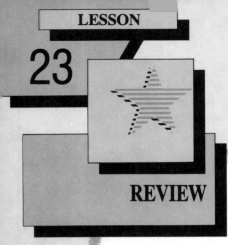

Ratio/Make a Table

A **ratio** is used to compare two quantities.

You can compare two parts: 3 striped scarves to 6 plaid scarves or
1 striped scarf to every 2 plaid scarves

You can compare 1 part and the whole: 3 striped scraves to 9 scarves
or 1 striped scarf to every
3 scarves

Complete the tables.

1. 3 red cars for every 5 blue cars

Red cars	3	6	9	12	15
Blue cars	5				

2. 5 girls for every 7 boys

Girls	5	10	15	20	25
Boys	7				

3. 4 out of every 10 people have brown hair

Brown Haired People		4		
Total people		10	20	30

Fill in the values for these ratios.

4. 1 pencil weighs 8 grams

Pencils							
Grams							

5. 3 rubber bands weigh 4 grams

Rubber bands						
Grams						

6. 2 peaches cost 50¢

Peaches							
Cost							

1. Complete the table.

Pounds of oranges	2	4		8	10	12	14
Cost					$16.00		

2. What is the price of 1 pound? _____

3. Explain how you found the price of 1 pound. _____

_____

4. If 3 pounds of oranges contain 12 oranges, how many oranges are contained in 10 pounds?

_____

5. What is the price of 1 orange? _____ How did you find this answer?

_____

A fifth grade class planted seeds to see if they would grow. Four out of every 6 seeds grew into a plant. Show this information on a table.

6. If you planted 120 seeds, how many plants would you expect to grow?

_____

7. If you wanted 200 plants, how many seeds should you plant?

_____

8. Explain how you used ratios to find the answers to exercises 6 and 7.

_____

_____

PROBLEM SOLVING
Make a Table

To check the quality of the coins minted at one United States mint in 1915, samples of coins were taken. One sample contained 2 dimes for every 3 pennies and had a value of $3.22. How many dimes were in the sample?

 Use estimation to help you find the answer.

1. If the sample contained 40 dimes, how many pennies were there?

_____

2. How did you decide that? _____

_____

_____

3. What would be the value of the dimes? _____

4. What would be the total value of the coins? _____

5. If the sample contained 12 pennies, how many dimes would it contain?

_____

6. How did you find that answer? _____

_____

_____

7. What would be the value of the sample of coins in exercise 5?

_____

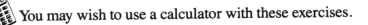

You may wish to use a calculator with these exercises.

8. Use the table below to find the coins that total $3.22. Use estimation to decide what other numbers to try.

Number of pennies	12					
Number of dimes	8					
Value of pennies	$.12					
Value of dimes	$.80					
Total value of coins	$.92					

At branding time there were 7 cattle for every 4 cowboys. If there are a total of 288 legs, how many cattle are there?

9. Make a table listing cattle, cowboys, and legs. Estimate to select values close to the correct answer.

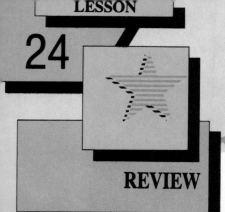

Ratio and Proportion/
Solve a Simpler Problem

When 2 ratios are equal, it is called a **proportion**.
Two ratios are equal if you can express them as equivalent fractions.

$\frac{2}{3} = \frac{n}{18}$ To make these two fractions equivalent and the ratios equal,
n must equal 12.

$\frac{2}{3} = \frac{12}{18}$ is a proportion.

Put an **X** in the squares containing equal ratios. Find a trail from start to finish.

START	$\frac{4}{16} = \frac{2}{8}$	$\frac{3}{5} = \frac{12}{20}$	$\frac{2}{7} = \frac{4}{14}$	$\frac{9}{8} = \frac{18}{16}$	$\frac{5}{10} = \frac{2}{5}$
$\frac{5}{6} = \frac{10}{18}$	$\frac{2}{3} = \frac{1}{6}$	$\frac{3}{7} = \frac{12}{21}$	$\frac{2}{4} = \frac{8}{4}$	$\frac{3}{5} = \frac{9}{20}$	$\frac{3}{4} = \frac{9}{12}$
$\frac{14}{12} = \frac{7}{2}$	$\frac{1}{8} = \frac{2}{4}$	$\frac{2}{9} = \frac{14}{63}$	$\frac{5}{3} = \frac{10}{6}$	$\frac{1}{6} = \frac{2}{12}$	$\frac{13}{15} = \frac{15}{13}$
$\frac{2}{6} = \frac{6}{12}$	$\frac{2}{3} = \frac{28}{42}$	$\frac{8}{13} = \frac{40}{55}$	$\frac{2}{9} = \frac{12}{45}$	$\frac{5}{4} = \frac{10}{2}$	$\frac{1}{13} = \frac{2}{29}$
$\frac{7}{3} = \frac{21}{6}$	$\frac{15}{3} = \frac{30}{9}$	$\frac{5}{13} = \frac{15}{39}$	$\frac{12}{8} = \frac{3}{2}$	$\frac{7}{8} = \frac{49}{56}$	FINISH

x   x   x   x   x   x   o   o   o   o   o   o   o   o   o

X   X   X   X   O   O   O   O   O   O

1. What is the ratio of Xs to Os in the first row? _____

2. What is the ratio of Xs to Os in the second row? _____

3. What is the ratio of Xs to Os in the entire array? _____

4. Are the ratios in exercises 1, 2, and 3 equal? _____

5. How do you know? _____

    _____

    _____

6. If you added 8 Xs to row 1, how many Os would you have to add to

    row 1 to maintain an equal ratio?_____

7. If you tripled the number of objects in row 2, what would be the ratio

    of Xs to Os? _____

8. If you multiplied the number of Os in the first row by 4, how many Xs

    would you have to add to keep the same ratio? _____

PROBLEM SOLVING

Solve a Simpler Problem

On an automobile trip, Malcolm and his brothers counted cows and horses to pass the time. When the trip was over, Malcolm discovered they had counted 5 cows for every 3 horses. If the total was 120 animals, how many horses did they count?

 Drawing a picture may help you understand the problem.

1. Draw a picture to show the ratio of cows and horses.

2. With 5 cows and 3 horses there are a total of eight animals. If you doubled the number of animals, would the ratio remain the same?

_____ Show this on your picture.

3. What would be the total number of animals? _____

4. What is the ratio of horses to total animals? _____

5. If there were 10 times as many animals as your diagram shows, how many horses would there be? (Remember the ratio must remain

the same.) _____

6. If there were 120 animals in all, how many horses would there be?

_____

To impress the science teacher, Carrie decided to make the largest bug collection in class. She worked hard crawling and climbing and searching. When she finally brought her collection to school, she had 5 beetles for every butterfly and 3 butterflies for every grasshopper. She had 4 other bugs that nobody could identify. If she had a total of 156 bugs, how many butterflies did she have?

7. What was the total number of beetles, butterflies, and

grasshoppers in her collection? _____

8. Draw a picture to show the ratio.

9. What was the number of grasshoppers in the collection? _____

10. How many butterflies did she have? _____

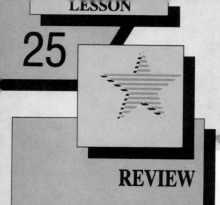

Solid Figures/
Make a Model

Solid figures contain **faces, corners,** and **edges.**
Flat surfaces are called **faces.**
Two or more faces join at an **edge.**
Edges join at a **corner.**

1. Complete the table.

Figure	Number of faces	Number of edges	Number of corners
Square Pyramid			
Cube			
Cylinder			
Triangular Prism			
Sphere			
Triangular Pyramid			

Look at these unfolded patterns for solids. List the number of faces, edges, and corners for each.

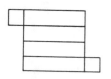

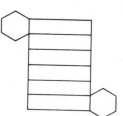

2. Faces _____   3. Faces _____   4. Faces _____

   Corners _____   Corners _____   Corners _____

   Edges _____   Edges _____   Edges _____

Use the clues to name each figure and make a sketch of it.

1. All four of my faces are flat. I look like a tent.

2. I am solid but not a prism. Some say I look like a silo.

_____

3. My base is a circle. My top is a point.

4. I have 6 faces. Each one is exactly the same.

_____

5. I am a solid, but not a prism. Polygons or circles are not part of my surface.

6. Some of my faces are shaped like rectangles. Two of my faces are shaped like triangles.

_____

PROBLEM SOLVING
Make a Model

Many houses in the 1950s were built with kits. The customer received panels in the shapes of rectangles or triangles which they connected to form the outside walls, the roof, and the floor of the house. A rectangular panel cost $1,500 and a triangular panel cost $1,000. The panels were connected with a special molding which cost $100 each. Mrs. Higgins wanted a house which looked like a pyramid on top of a cube. How much would that house cost?

1. Draw a picture of what that house would look like.

List information in an organized way to help you solve a problem.

2. Number of triangular panels
needed _____

3. Total cost of triangular
panels _____

4. Number of rectangular panels
needed _____

5. Total cost of rectangular
panels _____

6. Number of moldings
needed _____

7. Cost of molding _____

8. Total cost of this house _____

Looking at the Richardson house from the front you see:

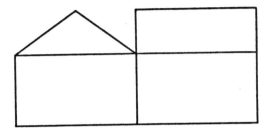

Looking at the Richardson house from the side you see:

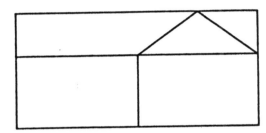

It costs an additional $200 to cut out a section of any panel. How much will it cost to build this home?

9. Rectangular panels _____ Cost _____

10. Triangular panels _____ Cost _____

11. Moldings _____ Cost _____

12. Cuts _____ Cost _____

13. Total Cost _____

14. Later the Richardson's added an addition on the left side of their house. This brought the total value of their home to $42,600. Draw a picture of what the house plus the addition looked like from the front.

Probability/Use a Picture

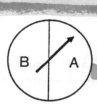

Alina spun the arrow
on this spinner.
The arrow points to **A**.

1. How many sections are on this spinner? _____

2. How many sections are marked with an **A**? _____

3. What is the probability of the arrow on
   this spinner pointing to **A**? _____

Darryl spun the arrow
on this spinner.
The arrow points to **C**.

4. How many sections are on this spinner? _____

5. How many sections are marked with a **C**? _____

6. How many sections are marked with a **D**? _____

7. What is the probability of the arrow on this spinner pointing to:

   C _____   **D** _____

8. Draw and label sections on this
   spinner so the probability of
   the arrow pointing to **E** is $\frac{2}{4}$,
   F is $\frac{1}{4}$, and **G** is $\frac{1}{4}$.

9. Draw and label sections on this
   spinner so the probability of
   the arrow pointing to **B** is $\frac{1}{8}$,
   C is $\frac{1}{2}$, and **D** is $\frac{3}{8}$.

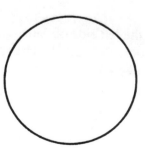

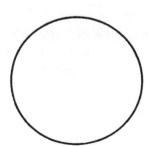

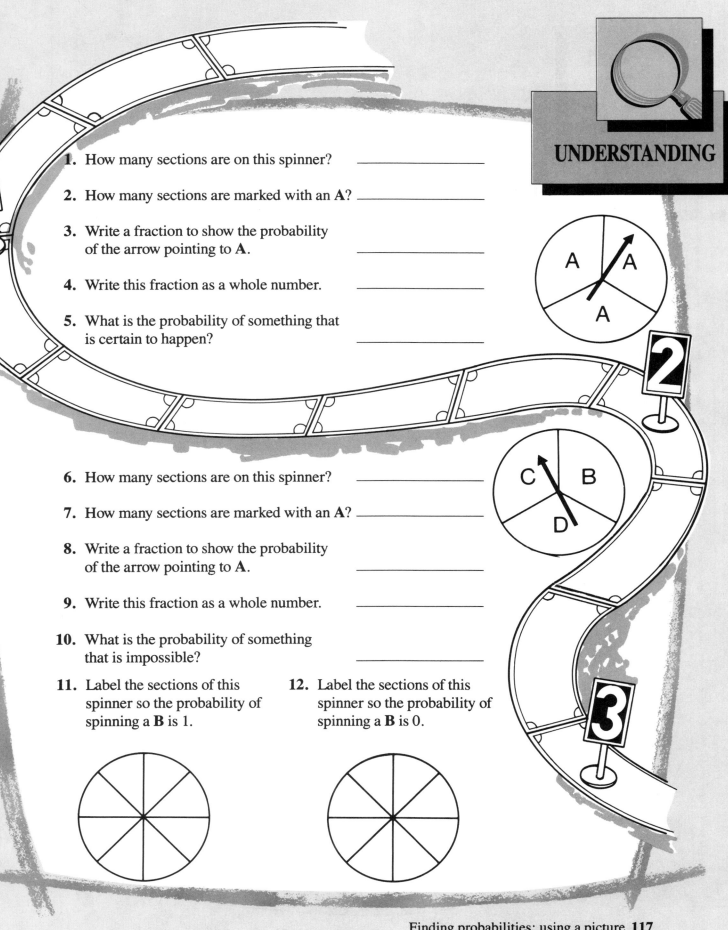

1. How many sections are on this spinner? _____

2. How many sections are marked with an **A**? _____

3. Write a fraction to show the probability of the arrow pointing to **A**. _____

4. Write this fraction as a whole number. _____

5. What is the probability of something that is certain to happen? _____

6. How many sections are on this spinner? _____

7. How many sections are marked with an **A**? _____

8. Write a fraction to show the probability of the arrow pointing to **A**. _____

9. Write this fraction as a whole number. _____

10. What is the probability of something that is impossible? _____

11. Label the sections of this spinner so the probability of spinning a **B** is 1.

12. Label the sections of this spinner so the probability of spinning a **B** is 0.

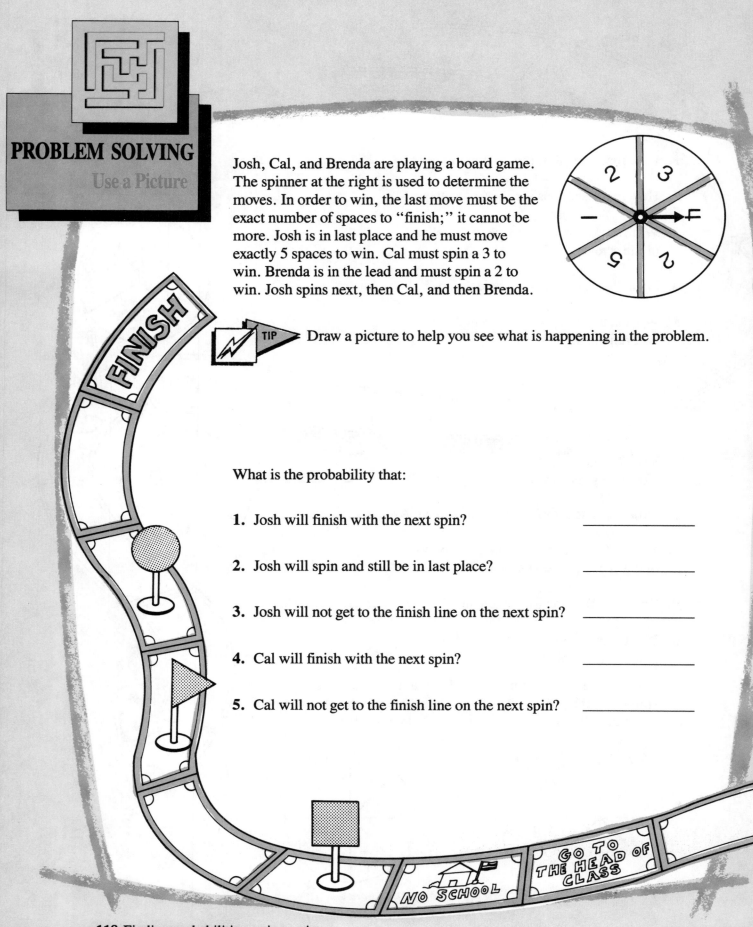

PROBLEM SOLVING
Use a Picture

Josh, Cal, and Brenda are playing a board game. The spinner at the right is used to determine the moves. In order to win, the last move must be the exact number of spaces to "finish;" it cannot be more. Josh is in last place and he must move exactly 5 spaces to win. Cal must spin a 3 to win. Brenda is in the lead and must spin a 2 to win. Josh spins next, then Cal, and then Brenda.

TIP Draw a picture to help you see what is happening in the problem.

What is the probability that:

1. Josh will finish with the next spin? _____

2. Josh will spin and still be in last place? _____

3. Josh will not get to the finish line on the next spin? _____

4. Cal will finish with the next spin? _____

5. Cal will not get to the finish line on the next spin? _____

What is the probability that:

6. Brenda will finish with the next spin? _____

7. Brenda will not get to the finish line on the next spin? _____

8. Who has the best chance to win on the next spin? _____

Ralph, Tami, and Janelle are playing a board game. They spin in that order. The probability that Ralph will not spin exactly what he needs to finish on the next spin is $\frac{4}{6}$. The probability that Tami will spin just enough to catch up with Janelle is $\frac{1}{6}$. The probability that Janelle will spin exactly what she needs to finish is $\frac{3}{6}$. Study the spinner.

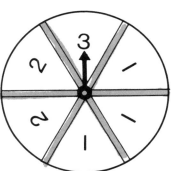

9. Draw their markers in the correct places on the game board.

Ralph ⬤   Tami ⬛   Janelle △

Ordered Pairs/
Read and Use a Graph

Name the ordered pair for each of the letters.

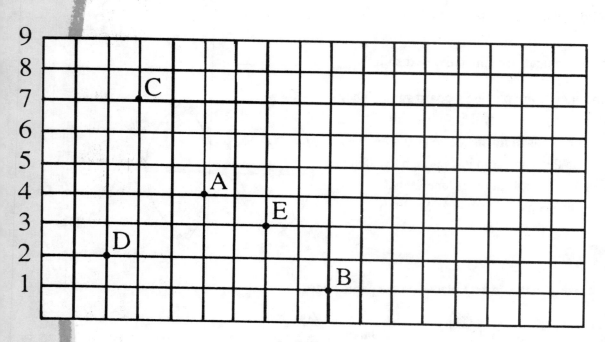

1. A. _____ **2.** B. _____ **3.** C. _____ **4.** D. _____ **5.** E. _____

Place the letters on the grid to show these ordered pairs.

6. F at (3,4)   **7.** G at (1,6)   **8.** H at (5,2)

9. I at (0,4)   **10.** J at (2,4)

11. Connect points A, H, D, and J. What shape is formed?

_____

12. Connect points I, C, E, and B. What shape is formed?

_____

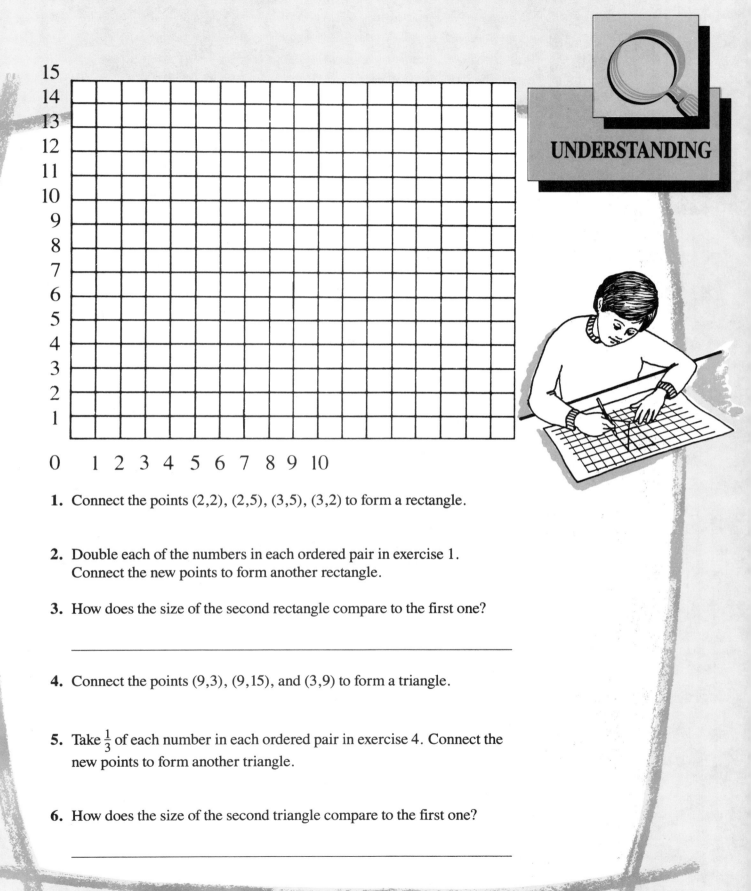

1. Connect the points (2,2), (2,5), (3,5), (3,2) to form a rectangle.

2. Double each of the numbers in each ordered pair in exercise 1. Connect the new points to form another rectangle.

3. How does the size of the second rectangle compare to the first one?

_____

4. Connect the points (9,3), (9,15), and (3,9) to form a triangle.

5. Take $\frac{1}{3}$ of each number in each ordered pair in exercise 4. Connect the new points to form another triangle.

6. How does the size of the second triangle compare to the first one?

_____

PROBLEM SOLVING
Read and Use a Graph

To keep the location of their silver mine a secret, the Dusty Gulch miners used a code. They drew a rectangle on the map. Then they wrote another ordered pair on the map. The secret to finding the mine was to start at the ordered pair and draw a rectangle 4 times as large, with sides parallel to the one shown. Then diagonals were drawn on the larger rectangle. The mine was located where the diagonals crossed. At which ordered pair was the mine located?

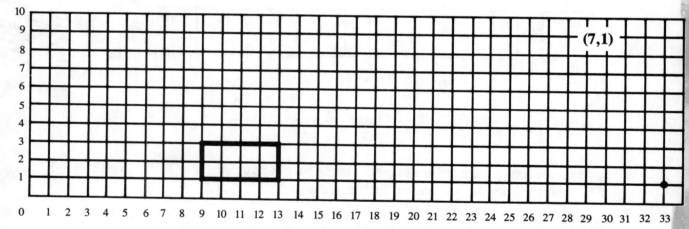

1. What are the ordered pairs of the given rectangle?

   _____ _____ _____ _____

2. What is the length of the rectangle? _____

3. What is the width of the rectangle? _____

4. If the unknown rectangle is 4 times as large, what is the length and width of that rectangle?

   Length _____   Width _____

5. Starting from the given point, draw in the length of the unknown rectangle.

6. Now draw in the width of the unknown rectangle.

7. Complete the drawing of the larger rectangle.

8. Connect the corners across the rectangle (diagonals).

9. What ordered pair lies at the intersection of those segments? _____

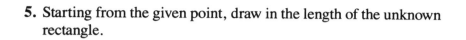 Carefully read the problem and plan each step of the solution.

Using a different code to find an ordered pair, another mine could be located on the same map. To find the first number, the miners tripled the first number of the ordered pair at the intersection of the diagonals on the small rectangle. The second was one-half of the second number of the ordered pair at the intersection of the diagonals on the large rectangle. Where was the mine located?

10. Draw in the diagonals of the small rectangle. What is the ordered pair

of the intersection? _____

11. What is the number pair that locates the mine? _____

12. Locate the mine on the map.

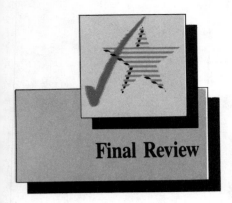

Final Review

DIRECTIONS:

Read each question. Choose the best answer. Mark that answer in the space provided at the bottom of the page.

1. What is the perimeter of this shape?

1) 11 units
2) 22 units
3) 28 units
4) 29 units
5) Not given

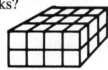

2. What is the volume of these blocks?

1) 6 cubic units
2) 15 cubic units
3) 24 cubic units
4) 28 cubic units
5) Not given

3. What should be the missing numbers in this table?

1	2	3	4	5
3				

1) 6, 9, 12, 15
2) 4, 8, 12, 16
3) 8, 16, 24, 32
4) 6, 12, 18, 24
5) Not given

4. If you folded this pattern into its solid shape, how many corners would it have?

1) 5
2) 6
3) 7
4) 10
5) Not given

5. What is the probability that a spinner will point to A?

1) $\frac{1}{4}$
2) $\frac{1}{3}$
3) $\frac{1}{2}$
4) $\frac{2}{3}$
5) Not given

6. What ordered pair is located at B?

1) (4,6)
2) (6,4)
3) (4,4)
4) (6,6)
5) Not given

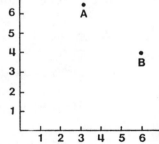

1. ① ② ③ ④ ⑤
2. ① ② ③ ④ ⑤
3. ① ② ③ ④ ⑤

4. ① ② ③ ④ ⑤
5. ① ② ③ ④ ⑤
6. ① ② ③ ④ ⑤

7. What formula represents the area of the given shape?

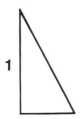

1) 1 + W
2) 1 + 1 + W + W
3) 1 × W
4) $\frac{1}{2}$ (1 × W)

8. What is the volume of a rectangular prism with dimensions twice as great as the one pictured?

1) 48
2) 36
3) 24
4) 12

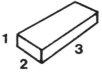

9. What solid figure is described below?
I have 5 faces. Only 1 of my faces is a square.

1) cube
2) square pyramid
3) rectangular prism
4) rectangular cylinder

10. If you added 6 more triangles to those pictured below, how many squares would you need to add to retain an equal ratio?

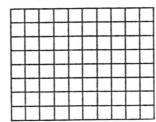

1) 4
2) 6
3) 8
4) 12

11. Which of the following is least likely to occur?
1) It will be cloudy today.
2) You will toss a coin 4 times and it will come up heads each time.
3. You will get a B on a test.
4. The sun will rise in the west.

12. What are the ordered pairs of the corners of a rectangle with a length of 6 units and a width of 4 units?

1) (1,4), (1,7), (7,7), (7,4)
2) (4,6), (4,4), (6,4), (6,6)
3) (2,5), (9,5), (6,3), (5,6)
4) (2,3), (6,3), (6,9), (2,2)

7. ① ② ③ ④
8. ① ② ③ ④
9. ① ② ③ ④

10. ① ② ③ ④
11. ① ② ③ ④
12. ① ② ③ ④

13. How many small rectangles, each 5cm × 8cm, can fit into a large rectangle 30cm × 40cm?

1) 5
2) 6
3) 30
4) 120

14. Forty-eight squares of equal size are exactly fitted into a rectangle 9 ft × 12 ft. What is the length of each side of the square?

1) 6 in.
2) 12 in.
3) 16 in.
4) 18 in.

15. The shape shown below would cost $4.50. If each _____ costs 15¢, what is the cost of each ▭ ?

1) $4.00
2) $1.20
3) $0.45
4) $0.30

16. A taxi driver charges $1.50 for the first $\frac{1}{4}$ mile and 50¢ for each $\frac{1}{4}$ mile after that. How much would it cost to ride $6\frac{1}{2}$ miles?

1) $6.50
2) $12.50
3) $14.00
4) $15.50

17. A rectangular prism 3 × 6 × 4 is made up of 72 cubes. The outside of the prism is painted. How many of the 72 cubes are not painted?

1) 4
2) 8
3) 12
4) 16

18. A cube with 3 units along each edge is made into a cube 5 units along each edge by adding unit cubes. How many cubes are added?

1) 8
2) 27
3) 98
4) 125

13. ① ② ③ ④
14. ① ② ③ ④
15. ① ② ③ ④

16. ① ② ③ ④
17. ① ② ③ ④
18. ① ② ③ ④

19. Maria has 3 pennies for every quarter. She has a total of $1.96. How many quarters does she have?

1) 3
2) 5
3) 7
4) 9

20. There are 3 times as many dogs as boys playing in the yard. If there are a total of 112 legs, how many dogs are there?

1) 24
2) 30
3) 34
4) 56

21. Opal is 3 marks away from the finish line in a board game. She can win if she spins a 3 or more. What is the probability that she will win using the spinner below?

1) $\frac{1}{6}$
2) $\frac{1}{3}$
3) $\frac{1}{2}$
4) 1

22. Rod is 2 spaces from the finish on a game board. His chances of spinning a number of 2 or more are 4 out of 6. Which of the spinners below is he using?

1)

2)

3)

4)

23. In a school there were 4 girls to every 5 boys. If there were a total of 360 students in the school, how many boys were there?

1) 90
2) 120
3) 150
4) 200

19. ① ② ③ ④
20. ① ② ③ ④
21. ① ② ③ ④

22. ① ② ③ ④
23. ① ② ③ ④